In *Mourning Becomes the Law*, Gillian Rose takes us beyond the impasse of post-modernism or 'despairing rationalism without reason'. Arguing that the post-modern search for a 'new ethics' and ironic philosophy are incoherent, she breathes new life into the debates concerning power and domination, transcendence and eternity.

Mourning Becomes the Law is the philosophical counterpart to Gillian Rose's highly acclaimed memoir *Love's Work*. She extends similar clarity and insight to discussions of architecture, cinema, painting and poetry, through which relations between the formation of the individual and the theory of justice are connected. At the heart of this reconnection lies a reflection on the significance of the Holocaust and Judaism.

Mourning Becomes the Law reinvents the classical analogy of the soul, the city and the sacred. It returns philosophy, Nietzsche's 'bestowing virtue', to the pulse of our intellectual and political culture.

MOURNING BECOMES THE LAW

'I may die before my time', Gillian Rose says in this remarkable book. She did; but she understood dying as few people have, and she lived her drastically shortened time as a philosopher who believed both in the soul and in the necessary charm of earthly powers. The just city, for Gillian Rose, is not built by the abandonment of reason or the proclamation of uncompromised virtue. It is built by faith in the achievements of even ruined reason and in the different chances of politics that are not ashamed of themselves. Death is at the heart of this book, but no one has ever argued more beautifully or eloquently that "death is not for nothing", and that mourning, when it becomes the law, that is, when it returns to reason, could even put an end to what Gillian Rose calls the "endless dying" of life under tyranny.'

Michael Wood, Princeton University

'*Mourning Becomes the Law* extends and deepens Gillian Rose's critique of postmodernism, especially in its "ethical" guise. She demonstrates the complicity between a "holocaust piety", an escapist fantasy concerning a misrepresented Judaism, and a fetishization of death. This book heralds a new theoretical dawn.'

John Milbank, University of Cambridge

MOURNING
BECOMES THE LAW

Philosophy and Representation

GILLIAN ROSE

CAMBRIDGE
UNIVERSITY PRESS

Published by the Press Syndicate of the University of Cambridge
The Pitt Building, Trumpington Street, Cambridge CB2 IRP
40 West 20th Street, New York, NY 10011–4211, USA
10 Stamford Road, Oakleigh, Melbourne 3166, Australia

First published 1996
Reprinted 1997

Printed in Great Britain at the University Press, Cambridge

A catalogue record for this book is available from the British Library

Library of Congress cataloguing in publication data applied for

ISBN 0 521 57045 X hardback
ISBN 0 521 57849 3 paperback

SE

CONTENTS

vii

Introduction

It is strange to live in a time when philosophy has found so many ways to damage if not to destroy itself. One by one all of the classical preoccupations of philosophy have been discredited and discarded: eternity, reason, truth, representation, justice, freedom, beauty and the Good. The dismissal of 'metaphysics' is accompanied by the unabated search for a *new ethics*. Yet no one seems to have considered what philosophical resources remain for an ethics when so much of the live tradition is disqualified and deadened.

From Marx to Heidegger (and before and beyond), it has become *de rigueur* to charge your predecessor with adherence to 'metaphysics', and to claim your 'new method' to be, exclusively and exhaustively, the overcoming of the tradition. Ethical integrity is reclaimed by each new generation who must murder their intellectual fathers in order to obtain the licence to practise the profession that they learnt from them. Today, fifty years after the end of the Second World War, three more or less buried strata of the post-war settlement suddenly demand attention and address: the Holocaust, Heidegger's Nazism, the disintegration of

I

Communism, perceived as the 'final' defeat of Marxism. To respond to this triple loss of authority, of Marxism, of Heideggerianism, and of our ability to come to terms with the Holocaust, by once again reviving the accusation that the Western philosophical tradition in general and modern philosophy in particular are 'metaphysical', and to resume once more the search for an uncontaminated ethics is to overlook the much more disturbing possibility that it may be the very severance of ethics from metaphysics that undermines the value and effectivity of both metaphysics and ethics. In both the world of politics and in the intellectual world, there seems to be a low tolerance of equivocation. The result of this intolerance and unease is the reproduction of dualistic ways of thinking and of formulating public policy. In philosophy 'truth' or 'reason', in their perennial or in their modern meanings, are charged with legitimising forms of domination which have destroyed or suppressed their 'others' in the name of the universal interest. *Pari passu*, in politics, across the spectrum of Western political parties, there is a consensus that attributes the insufficiencies of welfare liberalism or socialism of the post-war period to waste of resources and bureaucratisation. The indictment is extended to the principle of government as such, whether in the name of the new libertarianism or the new communitarianism. Why is it that a perceived equivocation or drawback, whether in 'reason' or 'truth' or 'welfare', results in an apparently wholesale rejection of the principle involved? You would expect the discovery of a limitation to require thorough analysis of principle and practice, so that the strengths and shortcomings of ideas and policies may be revised or modified in the light of experience. Wisdom, theoretical and practical, develops when the different outcomes of ideas and policies are related to the predictable modifications and to the unpredictable contingencies affecting their meaning and employment. Wisdom works with equivocation.

The unsparing revulsion against the fallen idols and the rush to espouse their formerly degraded 'others' perpetuate dualisms in which all the undesirable features of the original term are reinforced and reappear in its ostensibly newly revealed and valorised 'other'.

The current debate between liberals and communitarians in political philosophy, which translates at its extremes into the political polarisation of 'libertarians' and 'cultural or "ethnic" pluralism', displays the logic of this reversal. Liberals defend the autonomy and independence of the individual as conceived in the legal notion of human and civic 'rights', across the range of social and political meanings from 'entitlement' to 'free choice', while communitarians draw attention to the embeddedness of individuals in networks of shared meanings and social norms. The recent debate revives the eighteenth- and nineteenth-century debate over the radical rights enshrined in the French Revolution which provoked the conservative response based on custom and tradition. One can hear echoes of Kant versus Herder, Paine versus Burke or Sieyès and Renan, over the nature of political nationality: whether the voluntary association of free individuals constitutes the polity, or whether the organic community resting on history, territory, language and custom, cements the social and political bond. 'Libertarians' and 'cultural pluralists' derive institutional consequences from these opposed theoretical positions. The 'libertarian' argues for the minimal state and minimal taxes, leaving the greatest possible range of decisions and resources to the 'free' choice of the individual. An extreme version of this standpoint argues that even law and order should be privatised. 'Cultural pluralists' argue that political identity is no longer formed by class interests and allegiance. The post-colonial fragmentation of modern societies has given rise to diverse 'ethnic' communalities, based on 'race', religion, language, and gender constituencies. This perception justifies 'identity politics', the promotion of preferential legislation to redress and advance the 'empowerment' of previously disadvantaged cultural 'categories' of people. Intellectually, the political spectrum is divided between these alternatives: between the arbitrariness of the 'libertarian' individual and the arbitrariness of the 'communitarian' interest group.

Now, these two apparently warring engagements have a lot in common; and they participate in the very archetype which they claim to overthrow: the proto-rationality of a prescriptive political totality, justified as the fulfilment of history, truth, freedom and justice – as the unity of metaphysics and ethics. By maligning all putative universality as 'totalitarian' and seeking to liberate the 'individual' or the 'plurality' from domination, both the libertarian and the communitarian disqualify themselves from any understanding of the actualities of structure and authority, intrinsic to any conceivable social and political constitution and which their opposed stances still leave intact. The libertarian argument presupposes formal-legal rationality, just as the communitarian argument presupposes traditional rationality; both are types of legitimising domination as authority. Politics begins not when you organise to defend an individual or particular or local interest, but when you organise to further the 'general' interest within which your particular interest may be represented. As a result of this shared refusal to take responsibility for what Weber called the 'legitimate violences' of modern politics, libertarianism and communitarianism require other agencies to act on their behalf. Libertarian extensions of the right of 'individuals', the right to purchase and consume goods and services, presuppose and widen the already unequal distribution of opportunities and resources within a capitalist society. Extension of individual rights amounts to an extension not an attenuation of coercion: it calls for a reinforcement of the police function to contain the consequences of inequality. Communitarian empowerment of 'ethnic' and gender pluralities presupposes and fixes a given distribution of 'identities' in a radically dynamic society. 'Empowerment' legitimises the potential tyranny of the local or particular community in its relations with its members and at the boundary with competing interests. It is the abused who become the abusers; no one and no community is exempt from the paradoxes of 'empowerment'.

In their abstract and general opposition to the state, power, rationality and truth, libertarianism and communitarianism directly and indirectly aid and abet authoritarian power of control. They do so directly, by disowning the coercive immediacy of the type of action legitimated, and indirectly, in the way the stance at stake disowns the political implications of legitimated violence and so re-imposes that burden on agents and agencies of the state. These reversals in the planned reconfiguration of power arise from the attempt to develop normative political alternatives to the modern state without any preliminary analysis of the actualities and possibilities for freedom and justice. Any account of 'freedom' and 'justice' is deemed to depend on the 'metaphysics' of truth. When 'metaphysics' is separated from ethics in this way, the result will be unanticipated political paradoxes.

One recent version of this separation of metaphysics from ethics understands itself as a 'neo-pragmatics'. It deliberately eschews any theory of justice, for all such theories are said to be dependent on the metaphysics of objective truth independent of language. The pernicious holism of truth is attributed to the modern tradition whereby the theory of subjectivity, the theory of the freedom of the individual, is regarded as the basis of the possibility of collective freedom and justice. Cast as generally as this, the indictment of liberal metaphysics also applies to corporatist, and to revolutionary theories, and, in effect, to the overcoming of nihilism. In the place of this metaphysical tradition the 'creation of self' is to be explored independently of any theory of justice, which is thereby restricted to the vaporous ethics of 'cruelty' limitation, learnt from modern literature and not from analysis or philosophy. This separation of the self from any theoretical account of justice is advertised as a 'neo-pragmatics' for it claims to follow the contours of contingency and to avoid all and any structures of prejudged truth. Commitment to the ineluctable contingencies of language, self and community is presented as 'ironism' by contrast with liberal, metaphysical 'rationalism'. 'Ironism', the celebration of the sheer promiscuity of all intellectual endeavour, depends on this opposition to any philosophical position which presupposes an independent reality to which its conceptuality aims to be in some sense adequate.

However, there is nothing 'ironic' about this outmoded and dualistic contrast between the embrace of the contingency of language versus commitment to objective reality. Philosophy has practised what the early Romantic theorists called 'the irony of irony' since the beginning of the nineteenth century in recognition of the inevitable subjectivity of our positings, and of the ever-painful shifts to further positings of the relation between 'subjectivity' and 'objectivity', which always fail to guarantee a sustainable reality. The phenomenological 'irony of irony' expounds this drama of experience as intrinsically ironic: it acquires the doubled title by virtue of the expanded and implicated rationality of its expositions. Experience, expounded as the changing configurations of the inevitable collision between the concepts of self and reality, between concepts of subject and object, takes place moreover intersubjectively. It is conceptually impossible to produce a taxonomy which would sequester concepts of justice and the good from concepts of 'self-creation', for the very formation of 'selfhood' takes place in interaction with the mingled ethical and epistemological positings of the other, the partner in the formation of our contingent and unstable identities.

If libertarianism, with 'ironism' as one version, and cultural pluralism, with its new claimants for 'empowerment', may be dubbed 'post-modernism', then I describe 'post-modernism' as *despairing rationalism without reason*. Far from devastating and discarding rationality, each standpoint aims to redefine it, for otherwise no argument could be devised, no analysis could be conducted, and no conclusion could be urged. Yet, by disqualifying universal notions of justice, freedom, and the good, for being inveterately 'metaphysical', for colonising and suppressing their others with the violence consequent on the chimera of correspondence, 'post-modernism' has no imagination for its own implied ground in justice, freedom and the good. This ground is therefore held in a transcendence far off the ground, where, with a mixture of naivety and cynicism, without reason and in despair, post-modernism leaves analysed and unanalysed according to its tenets the pre-conditions and rampant consequences of power, domination and authority. 'Despairing rationalism without reason' is, I claim, the story of post-modernism. It is the story of what happens when 'metaphysics' is barred from ethics.

Philosophy as I practise it has a different orientation based on a different logic and a different story. From Plato to Marx, I would argue, it is always possible to take the claims and conceptuality of philosophical works (I say 'works' not 'texts': the former implying

the labour of the concept inseparable from its formal characteristics as opposed to the latter with its connotations of signifiers,
the symbolic and semiotics) *deterministically* or *aporetically* – as
fixed, closed conceptual structures, colonising being with the
garrison of thought; or according to the difficulty which the
conceptuality represents by leaving gaps and silences in the mode
of representation. These alternatives are well-known in the case of
Marx and Marxism. Marx's works can be interpreted deterministically: as formulating the iron laws of history from which the
inevitable outcome of class struggle in the victory of the proletariat
can be predicted. The same works can be interpreted aporetically:
as stressing the gap between theory and practice, which strain
towards each other; as insisting on the uncertain course of class
struggle, which depends on the unpredictable configurations of
objective conditions and the formation of class consciousness; as
imagining the multiplicity of eventualities which might emerge
between the extremes, 'Barbarism or Socialism'. Similarly, Plato's
dialogues may be interpreted deterministically or aporetically.
Both the Socratic dialogues and the non-Socratic dialogues can be
read according to the 'two-worlds' dogma: a world of transcendent, immutable, eternal Forms or prototypes, and the unreal,
mutable transient shadow world of types, which participate in the
eternal world. While the aporetic nature of Aristotle's thought has
been increasingly acknowledged in spite of its subsequent reduction to dogma by later Christian and Islamic thinkers, the parallel
point needs to be stressed for Plato. Few words occur as frequently
in the dialogues as 'aporia': it covers the difficulty of resolving,
even of clarifying philosophical investigations, or even of deciding
on the meaning of terms. Plato's aporia, like Aristotle's and
Aristotelianism, is displaced by the tradition of Platonism –
Plotinus, Proclus, Ficino.

If the 'Western tradition' were to be approached aporetically and not deterministically or dogmatically, then the relation between metaphysics and ethics would acquire a different resonance and rationale. The gap between Platonic type and archetype, between the Aristotelian universal, the particular and the irreducibly singular, is not expunged by the nostalgia for presence evident in the compensatory concatenations of representation. The gaps indicate the irruption of thought: not the irruption of the city, alternately legitimate and illegitimate in its monopoly of domination and authority, of the means of violence in the actuality of power, into the peaceful groves of thought, but the perceived breakdown of Athenian democracy as the precondition and pain of the existence of the Academy, galvanising the difficulty of thinking in the wake of disaster, without generating any fantasy of mending the world – even less of mending the 'two worlds'. According to this account, Plato is as 'realistic' about power, violence and domination as Thucydides; and Thuycydides' history serves as ethical an impulse as Plato's philosophy. Ethics and metaphysics are torn halves of an integral freedom to which they have *never* added up.

It is this classical reflection on the analogies between the soul, the city and the sacred, that I try in this work to renew and reinvent for our time, call it 'modernity' or 'post-modernity'. Of course, taken aporetically, that renewal is what I would argue most post-Kantian thinkers have aimed to develop. Here I include Hegel, Kierkegaard and Nietzsche equally with the sociological canon of Marx, Durkheim and Weber as analysts and dramatists of the capitalist and modern world. The sociologists, too, have railed against metaphysics while, in the name of scientific method, they have launched a new ethical endeavour in their sea of troubles and of difficulty.

The reflections to be developed here on the soul, the city and the sacred do not begin with a prerogative claim based on the suppression of 'the other', which installs repetitive dualisms of power and otherness within the protest against power. Here it takes three to make a relationship between two: the devastation between posited thought and posited being, between power and exclusion from power, implies the universal, the third partner, which allows us to recognise that devastation. The aporia or gap is the Janus-face of the universal. Together, universal and aporia are irruption and witness to the brokenness in the middle. This ethical witness, universal and aporetic, can only act with some dynamic and corrigible metaphysics of universal and singular, or archetype and type, or concept and intuition. The use of 'analogy' between the soul, the city and the sacred implies that the logic of these relationships has not been prejudged. The 'ana' expresses the gap, while the 'logy', the logos, makes it possible to speak, to propose to raise the difficulty of knowing or not knowing the relation between the three. 'The soul' suspends the modern philosophical command and intensity of 'subjectivity' while stressing the psychological and spiritual entity pervaded by the city and the sacred. 'The soul' is not a prisoner in the body (another travesty of Plato); the body is in the soul. 'The city' like 'the nation-state', implies the bounded political entity, but especially the breaches in its wall. 'The sacred', in its allusion to Marx's dictum, 'All criticism begins with the criticism of religion', picks up the paradox that the ignorance of this reality of the sacred and its ubiquitous reinsinuation now call for an explicit address. If the search for a new ethics divorced from 'metaphysics' to which post-modernism is devoted, has condemned itself to impotence and failure, then the missing resources may be found not in the dogma of truth but in the politics which has been disowned, and in the theology which has been more thoroughly suppressed. It is in the light of this expanding reflection on the soul, the city and the sacred that I introduce a reconsideration of 'the Holocaust' and of Judaism (chapters 1 and 5). I resist equally the super-eminence conferred on 'the Holocaust' as the logical outcome of Western metaphysical reason, and the unique status bestowed on Judaism as providing the communitarian and ethical integrity which otherwise lies in ruins in the 'post-modern world'. Instead I argue that rein-vigorated, open-hearted reason can discern a third city buried alive beneath the unequivocal opposition of degraded power and exalted ethics, Athens and Jerusalem (chapter 1). Then I argue that Judaism itself is best understood as a political and theological tradition, not as an ethical one. The uniqueness of the Rabbis in the post-Biblical formation of Judaism and in the subsequently changing pre-modern conditions was to mediate the relation between outer heteronomous power with inner, autonomous power. The internally contested meaning of law and power and ethics within modern Judaisms is examined on this basis. The arguments of each of these chapters demonstrate the invalidity of the opposition between liberal individualism and cultural pluralism.

Post-modernism in its renunciation of reason, power, and truth identifies itself as a process of endless mourning, lamenting the loss of securities which, on its own argument, were none such. Yet this everlasting melancholia accurately monitors the refusal to let go, which I express in the phrase describing post-modernism as 'despairing rationalism without reason'. One recent ironic aphor-ism for this static condition between desire for presence and acceptance of absence occurs in an interview by Derrida: 'I mourn, therefore I am'. By contrast *Mourning Becomes the Law* affirms that the reassessment of reason, gradually rediscovering its own moveable boundaries as it explores the boundaries of the soul, the city and the sacred, can complete its mourning. Completed mourning acknowledges the creative involvement of action in the configurations of power and law: it does not find itself unequivocally in a closed circuit which exclusively confers logic and power. In the title, *Mourning Becomes the Law*, 'Becomes' entertains the gradual process involved, and the connotation of 'suiting' or 'enhancing' the law in the overcoming of mourning. Meanwhile, like Elektra, mourning becomes Derrida. It is a tight fit. In chapter 4 I argue that Derrida's 'return' to Marx in the name of 'Spirit' amounts to another nail in the coffin of Marxism. Derrida's interpretation of Marx is structured by the Heideggerian conceptuality that he is truly mourning, while the notion he presents of 'the New International' reveals the anarchy and utopianism at the heart of the post-modern endeavour. I reopen the question of the relation between Hegel and Marx as a more fruitful way to reassess the resources of this tradition. Hegel is presented as a 'comic' thinker in order to provide a route into his thinking which bypasses the mines of prejudice concerning Hegel as a 'metaphysical' thinker.

The undermining of 'representation' is a further Heideggerian inheritance, prevalent in post-modern philosophy, and continuous with the maligning of metaphysics. Representation is said to depend on the assumption of a reality which is independent of language and thought, and is made 'present' in the reach and tropes of the traditional and modern cognitive claim. Now 'representation' has three domains: political representation, artistic representation and philosophical representation. The argument which would disband philosophical representation is applied equally to the issues omitted or suppressed in systems of political representation, and to any artistic activity based implicitly or explicitly on capturing reality. This is not simply the point that all forms of representation are conventional and not veridical; it is part of philosophy's more fundamental ambition to guard against any assumption of correspondence or adequation of thought and language to a world existing outside their confines. Yet this standpoint has its own naivety: it presents the 'metaphysical' commitment and its own 'irony' as the only two conceivable positions; and it still presupposes a cognitive stance whereby the single knower relocates the reality and status of what is known. If, however, 'reality' is intrinsically relational and experience is generated between what interconnected actors posit as independent of them and their difficult discovery of those positings, then the critique of representation becomes possible without it depending on any outworn metaphysical base. In chapter 2 and throughout this book I discuss architecture, painting, film and poetry in its representation of power, domination and the Holocaust. Alert to the critique of representation and to my own critique of that critique, I open up explorations of our mutual entanglements in power in a way which cannot be pursued when intellectual energy is devoted to the resistance to metaphysics, and, as a corollary, to one-dimensional conceptualisations of power.

The phenomenological description of experience implied in my approach contrasts with the sacrifice of any notion of experience in the various postmodern nostrums and 'ironies'. Without any necessary assumptions of linearity or progression, this alternative description of mutual positings and their breakdown also reopens the way to conceive learning, growth and knowledge as fallible and precarious, but risk-able. The risk refers to the temporarily constitutive positings of each other which form and reform both selves. This constant risk of positing and failing and positing again I call 'activity beyond activity', to cover the ethical nature of the description, and to distinguish it from the Levinasian 'passivity beyond passivity', the idea of ethics as the ego-less substitution of one for 'the other'. In chapter 5 I develop these concepts in an examination of the thought of Maurice Blanchot which seems to me to offer an extreme statement of many central post-modern themes.

Finally, in chapter 6, I tackle the Heideggerian reduction of eternity to finite being in the exposition of death. This reduction is all-pervasive in twentieth-century philosophical thought. To this reduction, which I argue goes against the grain of language and syntax, may be attributed many of the peculiarities of the Heideggerian style. Rumi and Rilke, my favourite poets, are here given – I hope not the last, but – the continuing word.

I

Athens and Jerusalem: a tale of three cities

I

We have given up communism – only to fall more deeply in love with the idea of 'the community'.

If 'communism' stood for an ideal community, what does the current idea of 'the community' stand for? Quite contrary things. Consider, we say, 'the European community', and we tried not to say, 'the community charge'; 'the American nation and community', says President Bill Clinton, but he also says, 'the politics of the community'. We say 'the community of nations', and we say, 'the ethnic community', and 'the religious community'. On the one hand, 'the community' retains its universal connotations of the common-wealth, the collective interest, the general will; on the other hand, 'the community' resounds with the particular connotations of the locality, the exclusive interests of specific people, the particular will. This exclusive 'community' implies traditional authority; that inclusive 'community' implies legal-rational authority.

Of course, in classic, liberal political theory, the constitution provides a structure of institutions to represent and mediate particular wills and the general will, to generate the commonwealth out of the clash of competing interests: from the premise of the sovereignty of the people emerges the theory of the representative modern state. In de Tocqueville's *Democracy in America*, the local community is held to be the source of tyranny; we have forgotten, too, that *Deutschland über alles* was originally intended to affirm the general, liberal state, based on universal rights, the *Rechtsstaat*, against the myriad regional jurisdictions of Princes and privileges.

Our new affirmation of the local community arises from our equal distrust of the spurious universality of the liberal state and of the imposed universal of the former state-socialisms, two ideals of political community. We judge and believe that both modernity and the critique of modernity have broken their promises. And yet we revert to *the equivocal promise* harboured in the idea of 'the community'.

What do we hope for from the ideal of the community?

We hope to solve the political problem; we hope for the *New Jerusalem*; we hope for a collective life without inner or outer boundaries, without obstacles or occlusions, within and between souls and within and between cities, without the perennial work which constantly legitimates and delegitimates the transformation of power into authority of different kinds.

Consider the case for community architecture, developed by Nick Wates and Charles Knevitt in their book published in 1987. Their case rests on the opposition between the evil empire and the perfect community, between *imperium* and ecclesiology, the perfect church. But who was to be the guarantor of this new community? Prince Charles.

All alien power is to be dissolved in community architecture: yet the regality and majesty of the 'popular' sovereign are needed to legitimise this proclaimed dissolution of power. In effect, all the paradoxes of power are transferred back into the community.

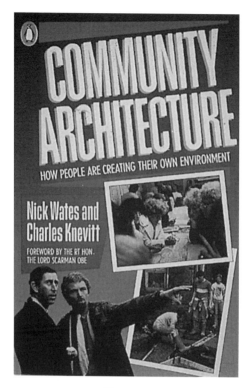

Figure 1

The argument for community architecture is summarised in a chart which appears in the book, entitled 'What Makes Community Architecture Different'. The chart sets out the contrasts between 'conventional architecture' and 'community architecture'.

For conventional architecture, the user is passive,
for community architecture, the user is active;

for conventional architecture, the expert is imperious,
for community architecture, the expert is companionable;

for conventional architecture, people are manipulated,
for community architecture, people manipulate the system;

conventional architecture is large-scale and requires wealth,
community architecture is small-scale and situated in decaying
locations;

conventional architecture has a single function,
community architecture serves plural functions;

conventional architecture draws on the international style and
employs cold technology,
community architecture draws on regional and vernacular
building traditions and employs convivial technology;

conventional architecture is preoccupied with financial and
political profit, community architecture is concerned with the
quality of life;

the ethos of conventional architecture is hieratic and
totalitarian,
the ethos of community architecture is demotic, mutual and
pragmatic.

Yet the cover of the book bears an image of Prince Charles, shoul-
der-to-shoulder with a casually dressed architect, whose emphatic
élan of arm and hand and pursed lip contrasts with the Prince's
corrugated forehead and incredulous, gaping mouth. These two
gesticulating figures appear freestanding against a background
montage of photographs, one of apparently ordinary women, who
are conversing over a table covered with architectural plans, and
the other of three, grubby, labouring lads, in what looks like an
ordinary backyard.

What is going on here? The argument throughout the book

seems to have an oppositional and dualistic structure: the idea of the community-in-architecture is developed in opposition to the coercive domination of modernist, bureaucratically managed, conventional architecture. Through every item on the stark list comparing conventional with community architecture, rationality is opposed to community, power abused is opposed to power dissolved and shared – old Athens is opposed to New Jerusalem. On the cover, the idea of a small-scale community, with no clash of particular wills, with, among the women, an ideal-speech situation, among the lads an ideal work situation, the idea of a non-coercive social cohesion, is insinuated by the montage of images. The idea of community depends, however, not only on its contraries, which are demonstrably attributed to conventional architecture, but also on the implied opposition of the community to the political and social totality. The inevitable political predicaments of sovereignty and representation have been projected beyond the boundaries of the community onto the presupposed but not thematised environing body-politic. Conceived without the politics of clashing interests and without the sociological actuality of how domination, including local domination, is to be legitimised as authority, all the oppositions held at bay in the chart will be reproduced within the community-in-architecture, and will take their revenge all the more for being unacknowledged.

The personality of the Prince is to provide the legitimating charisma for the community-in-architecture, as he rubs his *contrapposto* regal shoulder with the newly enhumbled expert – the architect. Could it be that this New Jerusalem is polluted by *the third city*, the fairy godmother who was not invited to this holy wedding of Prince and people? For does not each 'citizen' bear within herself two agonistic lives? As a member of civil society, she is legally autonomous and pursues her 'natural', individual and particular interests; and as a member of the community. she imagines her participation in a collectivity; she imagines it all the more when she is confronted by legitimate authority which seems to exclude her.

Doesn't community architecture encourage us to imagine a sham-community, a false Jerusalem? The opposition between the needs and interests of the people and 'conventional' architecture, the latter presented as continuous with the interest of the rationalised, coercive, modern state, is phantasmagorically overcome in the allegory of the Prince – the monarch-to-be serving his apprenticeship as the genie of every locality. Should we not in fact see ourselves in the architect, just as much as in the women or in the lads? The evils of civil society and of the state are merged in the figure of 'the architect', who takes on the anxiety of the separated life of each citizen – following his particular interests, he is vulnerable yet ruthless; aspiring to community, he is frail and self-fearing. An ethical immediacy, a community, is claimed for the people, while the separation between particular and universal is visible in the fraught bearing of the architect. And it is the architect who is demoted: the people do not accede to power.

II

I propose that, in the wake of deconstruction and post-modernism (how I wanted to write this lecture without letting those words pass my lips), we have lost all sureness of political discrimination. We no longer know where power resides – in social institutions? in organised knowledge? in the grand critiques of that knowledge? in ourselves, as will-to-power? The confusion in identifying the source and location of power goes together with the impossibility of analysing its structure. When a monolithic or plural character is attributed to power, conceived, for example, as patriarchal, this attribution perpetuates blindness to the reconfiguration of power which we may be assisting by our unarticulated characterisation of it.

It has become commonplace to argue that all social institutions, especially those based on knowledge, represent 'powers' (from the central state to local government, from professions – medicine, law, architecture – to the critical traditions in philosophy and in sociology). But by renouncing knowledge as power, we are then only able to demand expiation for total domination, for we have disqualified any possible investigation into the dynamics of the configuration and reconfiguration of power – which is our endless predicament. The presentation of power as plural yet total and all-pervasive, and of opposition to power thus conceived as equally pluralistic, multiform and incessant, as the anarchic community, unwittingly and unwillingly participates in a restructuring of power which undermines those semi-autonomous institutions, such as knowledge or architecture, which alleviate the pressure of the modern state on the individual. The plural but total way of conceiving power leaves the individual more not less exposed to the unmitigated power of the state.

Athens, the city of rational politics. has been abandoned: she is said to have proven that enlightenment is domination. Her former inhabitants have set off on a pilgrimage to the New Jerusalem, the imaginary community, where they seek to dedicate themselves to difference, to otherness, to love – to a new ethics, which overcomes the fusion of knowledge and power in the old Athens. What if the pilgrims, unbeknownst to themselves, carry along in their souls *the third city* – the city of capitalist private property and modern legal status? The city that separates each individual into a private, autonomous, competitive person, a bounded ego, and a phantasy life of community, a life of unbounded mutuality, a life without separation and its inevitable anxieties? A phantasy life which effectively destroys the remnant of political life?

Recently, I discovered a painting by Poussin, which illustrates the unintended consequences of our substitution of New Jerusalem for the missing analysis of old Athens. This substitution puts the idea of the community, of immediate ethical experience, in the place of the risks of critical rationality. Critical reason is discredited as domination, yet, at the same time, its authority, which was always drawn from absent but representable justice, is borrowed in the reduction to the immediate community or immediate experience.

Some of you may also have seen this painting not long ago. It was the first painting which was presented and discussed by Sister Wendy Beckett, in her recent series of ten-minute television programmes, 'Sister Wendy's Odyssey', on BBC 2. Now I don't want you to think that I do my research only by watching television. I had in fact attempted to video a film on ITV, but, instead of the film, which I was longing to watch, 'The Heart is a Lonely Hunter', I got – a nun.

What is more, Sister Wendy Beckett is an anchoress – she belongs to an order of nuns who permit her to live and eat alone. She has lived in a caravan by herself for twenty years, devouring fine art from postcards. The programmes follow her 'Odyssey', her first visits to galleries all over the country where the originals of her postcard reproductions are located. Anyone who has seen these programmes cannot fail to be struck by Sister Wendy's celebration of the entwining of human spirituality and human sexuality in the paintings she chose to present.

I was so struck by her discussion of the painting that I am going to show you, that I wrote to Sister Wendy, and attempted to set out my disagreements with what she said. To my delight, after several weeks, she replied, and we have entered into a lively correspondence on these and related matters.

The painting by Poussin, which hangs in the Walker Art Gallery, Liverpool, is called, *Gathering the Ashes of Phocion*. Poussin's source for the painting is Plutarch's *Life of Phocion*. According to Plutarch, Phocion was an Athenian general and statesman, who offered a model of civic virtue in his public and in his private life. During a period of deep unrest and political ferment in Athens, Phocion remained above reproach, and even refused the handsome benefices offered him by the king of Macedonia. He served as governor of Athens forty times, and often saved the city from destruction.

However, Phocion was eventually accused of treason by his enemies, and was sentenced to die, like Socrates, by taking hemlock. As an additional disgrace, Phocion's burial within Athens was forbidden, and no Athenian was to provide fire for his funeral. His body was taken outside the city walls and burnt by a paid alien; his ashes were left untended on the pyre.

In the middle of the story of Phocion, Plutarch introduces the character of Phocion's wife. Not named, she is, nevertheless, individuated by her virtue: her modesty and simplicity are said to have been as celebrated among Athenians as Phocion's integrity.

The painting shows Phocion's wife with a trusted woman companion. They have come to the place outside the city wall where the body of Phocion was burnt so that Phocion's wife may gather his ashes – for if they are left unconsecrated, his unappeased soul will wander forever. As she cannot bury the ashes in the tomb of his fathers, according to Plutarch, she takes the ashes

Figure 2 'Landscape with the Ashes of Phocion' by Poussin.
Published by kind permission of the Board of Trustees of the National Museums and
Galleries on Merseyside (Walker Art Gallery, Liverpool).

to her home and buries them by the hearth, dedicating them to the household gods. According to Sister Wendy – although I can't persuade her to reveal the source for this – Phocion's wife consumes the ashes of her disgraced husband, and thereby gives his unhappy soul a resting place, a tomb, in her own body.

Sister Wendy presented the gesture of the wife bending down to scoop up the ashes as an act of perfect love – as Jerusalem. She contrasted this gesture of love with the unjust nature of the city of Athens, which she saw represented in the classical architecture of the buildings, rising up in the combined landscape and cityscape behind the two women. According to this argument, the classical orders as such stand for the tyranny of the city of Athens. In this presentation of the rational order in itself as unjust power, and the opposition of this domination to the pathos of redeeming love, I discerned the familiar argument that all boundaries of knowledge and power, of soul and city, amount to illegitimate force, and are to be surpassed by the new ethics of unbounded community.

To oppose the act of redeeming love to the implacable domination of architectural and political order – here, pure, individual love to the impure injustice of the world – is completely to efface the politics of this painting.

Phocion's condemnation and manner of dying were the result of tyranny temporarily usurping good rule in the city. The tension of political defiance appears here in the figure of the woman servant, whose contorted posture expresses the fear of being discovered. The bearing of the servant displays the political risk; her visible apprehension protects the complete vulnerability of her mourning mistress as she devotes her whole body to retrieving the ashes. This act is not therefore solely one of infinite love: it is a finite act of political justice.

The magnificent, gleaming, classical buildings, which frame and focus this political act, convey no malignant foreboding, but are perfect displays of the architectural orders: they do not and cannot in themselves stand for the unjust city or for intrinsically unjust law. On the contrary, they present the rational order which throws into relief the specific act of injustice perpetrated by the current representatives of the city – an act which takes place outside the boundary wall of the built city.

The gathering of the ashes is a protest against arbitrary power; it is not a protest against power and law as such. To oppose anarchic, individual love or good to civil or public ill is to deny the third which gives meaning to both – this is the other meaning of *the third city* – the just city and just act, the just man and the just woman. In Poussin's painting, this transcendent but mournable justice is configured, its absence given presence, in the architectural perspective which frames and focuses the enacted justice of the two women.

To see the built forms themselves as ciphers of the unjust city has political consequences: it perpetuates endless dying and endless tyranny, and it ruins the possibility of political action.

That is what I wrote to Sister Wendy.

III

New Jerusalem, the new ethics, has been developed from a dangerously distorted and idealised presentation of Judaism as the sublime other of modernity. I shall return to this later. At the same time, a fourth city, emblem of contemporaneous Jewish history and now of modernity as such, has emerged from the ruin of theoretical and practical reason to provide the measure for demonic anti-reason – the city of Auschwitz.

Now, how can Auschwitz, the death camp of death camps, be a city? Philosophical, sociological, and architectural work on modernity and the Holocaust displays an intensification of the opposition between Athens and Jerusalem. Much of this work judges that generalising explanations are in themselves a kind of collusion in what should not be explained but should be left as an evil, unique in human and in divine history; and it calls for silent witness in the face of absolute horror. But to name the Nazi genocide 'the Holocaust' is already to over-unify it and to sacralize it, to see it as providential purpose – for in the Hebrew scriptures, a *holocaust* refers to a burnt sacrifice which is offered in its entirety to God without any part of it being consumed. The familiar structure of argument then runs as follows: a tight fit is posited between the Holocaust and a general feature of modernity – its legal-rationality, its architectural history, the logic of meaning itself. This leads to the judgement that the feature in question made the Holocaust possible or realisable. Sociologists, architectural historians and philosophers conclude that the methods and means of their own disciplines are principal actors in the Holocaust. The devastation of the respective discipline is declaimed; paradoxically, the sociologist then invokes the new ethics, the philosopher turns to social analysis, and the architectural historian breaks off his book after 500 pages, and relapses into a desperate, dramatised silence.

In each case, the same reversal of logic has occurred: critical rationality conceives and organises the investigation and provides the causal or conditional arguments which are developed in the light of the relevant historical evidence; for example, architectural planning and architects were crucial for the conception, organisation and execution of the Holocaust. Then the roles are reversed: the protagonist, reason, becomes the antagonist, anti-reason. The Holocaust is now seen as the immanent telos of those procedures, and itself becomes the measure, the limit, the criterion, of the invalidity of those modes of organised thinking; for example, the Holocaust demonstrates the corruption and corruptibility of the architectural tradition from the classical Athenian orders to the modern movement. Reason is revealed by the Holocaust to be contaminated, and the great contaminator, the Holocaust itself, becomes the actuality against which the history, methods and results hitherto of reason are assessed. The Holocaust provides the standard for demonic anti-reason; and the Holocaust founds the call for the new ethics.

In the architectural version of this argument developed by Robert Jan van Pelt in his book written with Westfall, *Architectural Principles in the Age of Historicism* (1991), Auschwitz plays a special role. At the other five death camps in Poland, all the buildings were destroyed by the Nazis; at Auschwitz, the only death camp which was also a labour camp, 250 buildings or their remnants remain to this day. The Nazi retreat in the face of the advancing Russian army was too hurried for them to be destroyed – only the four crematoria were blown up. In the architectural argument, Auschwitz is called a 'post-historical city', and is shown gruesomely to fulfil the five functions of the classic model of the five-square city – Athens. These five functions are said to be veneration of the dead, celebration of the future, government, which concerns the active present, dwelling, which concerns the passive present, and sustenance or trade. In the same order, the Athenian *stelai* or grave markers are said to correspond to the Nazi racial laws; the *acropolis* or shrine is said to correspond to the crematoria; the *agora, stoa* or *portico* are said to correspond to the roll calls; the *domus* is said to correspond to the barracks; the *taberna* or *emporium* to the part of the camp known by the inmates as Kanada, because it was the store for the precious belongings brought with them on the transports by Jews who believed that they were to be settled in new lands, in new communities. I shall return to assess this strange, functional argument later.

Since 1990, I have been acting as one of a number of consultants to the Polish Commission for the Future of Auschwitz – a deeply equivocal nomenclature. This Commission was set up by the Polish Ministry for Culture in 1990, when the Polish government had just taken over the running of the museum and site of Auschwitz from the Soviet Union for the first time since the end of the war. Our continuing brief, in meetings which have taken place in Oxford, Krakow and Auschwitz, has been twofold. One, to advise the museum staff on the restructuring of the museum at Auschwitz I. The exhibitions in the former barracks have remained unchanged for thirty-six years and were originally designed to document Nazi crimes in a way which legitimised Soviet Communism. Two, to advise on the organisation of visits to Auschwitz II Birkenau, the twenty-acre camp, three kilometres from Auschwitz I, with the infamous selection ramp, men's and women's camps, and the ruins of the four crematoria, built by the Nazis from scratch on the site of the demolished Polish village of Bzezinska.

On average, there are 750,000 visitors a year to Auschwitz, the overwhelming majority of them teenagers. No one under the age of thirteen is allowed on the site. We have been asked to reconsider the balance of cognitive, political, emotional and spiritual experience, which might be induced by the way a visit to the camp is organised. This reflection needs to be translated into the exhibitions at the museum at Auschwitz I and into the way visits are routed through Auschwitz II Birkenau. As it is currently organised, the main exhibition at the museum traumatises people so much that they never get to Birkenau, or if they do, they spend very little time there, even though it is by far the more important site.

This work at Auschwitz, 'the future of Auschwitz', raises in an acutely direct and practical way the question of the relation between knowledge and power. Are our attempts at independent critical reflection merely another stage in the culture industry which Auschwitz has become? While each consultant was invited on an individual and international basis, we soon became aware that our work is taking place in a theatre where Polish, American and Israeli interests clash. A number of Holocaust museums are currently being opened in America, the grandest of which in Washington DC was opened last year. We were horrified to learn that these museums have been outbidding each other for the acquisition of the last remaining, original, wooden barrack from Auschwitz-Birkenau. The Holocaust has become a civil religion in the United States, with Auschwitz as the anti-city of the American political community.

Working at Auschwitz has, however, convinced me that the apparently unnegotiable and expiatory opposition between reason and witness, between knowledge/power and new ethics, or between relativising explanation and prayer, protects us from confronting something even more painful, which is our persistent and persisting dilemma, and not something we can project onto a one-dimensional, demonic rationality, which we think we have disowned. New Jerusalem, the second city, is to arise out of Auschwitz, the fourth city, which is seen as the burning cousin – not the pale – of the first city, Athens. Might not this drama of colliding cities cover a deeper evasion – fear of a different kind of continuity between *the third city* and Auschwitz, which itself gives rise to the ill-fated twins of the devastation of reason and the phantasmagoric ethics of the community? For the perfection of the idealism of the political community is at the same time the perfection of the devastation of theoretical reason and of political action.

IV

Let us approach *this third city* by reconsidering the fourth city: Auschwitz. A Dutch colleague of mine, who now teaches in Canada, Robert Jan van Pelt, recently spent three months working in the archives of the museum at Auschwitz and living in the town of Oswiecim. Oswiecim is the Polish name for Auschwitz. However, it acquired its German name around 1272 and re-acquired it when it became part of the Austro-Hungarian empire. Auschwitz I was originally a barrack of the Polish army, a cluster of thirty or so well-constructed, brick buildings on the main road out of the town of Auschwitz. The Nazis took over the buildings, added a further brick storey to each and installed the perimeter fencing with the infamous watch-towers. As, today, you drive through the Polish town of Oswiecim, you suddenly come to the Nazi quarter (now inhabited by Poles). It is a town within a town, built in the German vernacular, with homes, schools, churches and a market, a stage-set phantasy of an idealised, *gemütlich*, familiar, German community.

In the museum itself, my colleague opened and analysed 300 archival boxes of architectural plans which have not been seen since the War – no architectural historian has worked at Auschwitz. Van Pelt has discovered that, before the Nazis began to lose the war, they had prepared plans for the town of Auschwitz to be developed into a major German city. Auschwitz was to become the administrative centre for the Germanification of eastern Upper Silesia, in the Nazi version of the medieval German ambition to civilise the Slav lands by colonising the territories between the River Oder and the River Bug. The problem which

31

Max Weber analysed in his famous essay, *Capitalism and Rural Society in Germany*, of replacing the large, moribund, Junker estates of the East with a small-holding, vigorous, independent peasantry, was to be solved by transferring peasant families from Germany through Auschwitz to establish this new blueprint of land tenure to the east. Auschwitz was chosen for this role because of its situation at the hub of railway connections which ramified across Europe – which was why Auschwitz, rather than the other five death-camps in Poland, became the destination for transports of Jews from all over Europe. Unlike the other Polish camps, Auschwitz was planned primarily as a labour camp, and it continued to operate as a labour camp throughout the war.

The extent of the planning was demonstrated by van Pelt last term when he visited Warwick University; he spent three hours showing my MA students, who are taking a course in Holocaust sociology and theology, about 200 slides of plans and photographic material from the museum archive. We saw plans for the Germanification of nature – Polish forests were to be replanted with German trees; plans for German dog-kennels for German dogs; designs for German arm-chairs for off-duty German officials. We saw photographs of German soldiers with large canisters of chemicals fumigating the former houses of Jews who had been transported further east – it was called ethnic cleansing – and then we saw normal, happy, German peasant families sitting comfortably and securely in their new homes. We also heard evidence of inefficiency: of the poor design of barracks causing unplanned disease and death; of theft and improvisation by the Nazis, necessitated by the deficient supply of barbed wire for the perimeter fencing.

Now the argument which might be developed from this kind of evidence that Auschwitz qualifies as a city has a fundamentally different logical structure from the strange argument, which I outlined earlier, that the five functions of the classical city of Athens have their functional equivalent in the organisation of Auschwitz as a death-camp, with the conclusion that the project of classical architecture and of architecture as such is implicated and condemned by Auschwitz. That argument, I suggested, sets Auschwitz up as the measure for demonic anti-reason. It rests on a dubious premise: that the meaning of the city is to be defined transhistorically, according to listed functions, rather than historically, according to the rule of law. According to the functional approach, the built types or forms of the city are classified by their eternally fixed function; according to the approach which would see the city as requiring the rule of law, the variable types and styles of building could be analysed as re-presenting the changing configuration of power and its legitimation. There was no rule of law at Auschwitz; and so, while the camp can be analysed as a social system – for the overthrow of normal expectations by the unpredictable mix of rules and terror required the socialisation of both SS and prisoners into a hierarchy of brutality – Auschwitz cannot be functionalised as a city.

The plans for Auschwitz as the administrative centre for the Germanification of central Poland present a different challenge. These scores of unrealised plans cannot be simply understood as the indictment and condemnation of classic architecture, modern planning or modern rationality as such. That is too easy, and, I want to argue, in its blanket condemnation, too exculpatory, for it eliminates the possibility of any specific investigation into the contingencies of collusion by making collusion already a foregone conclusion. Instead, the plans can be analysed, first, in terms of the attempt to legitimise a colonisation which has a long history in the relation between German capitalism and land tenure in the east, and an even longer history in the German medieval mission to the Slavs. Secondly, they can be analysed in terms of the emphasis on political community – the cosy German quarters in Oswiecim, the planned communities of German warrior-peasants in the east which, it was calculated, would have to defend their newly acquired land by force for generations against the Soviet Union. Thirdly, the plans can be analysed in terms of a reassessment of the identity of Auschwitz as a camp: it was designed to provide an endless supply of human slave-labour, and, according to van Pelt, became only secondarily a death camp, when the fresh supplies of labour included persons not suited for work.

Analysis of this kind, as opposed to the refusal of analysis implicit in the demonising argument, does not see Auschwitz as the end-product and telos of modern rationality. It understands the plans as arising out of, and as falling back into, the ambitions and the tensions, the utopianism and the violence, the reason and the muddle, which is the outcome of the struggle between the politics and the anti-politics of the city. This is *the third city* – the city in which we all live and with which we are too familiar.

Although van Pelt's work is as yet unpublished – he hopes it will be ready for the fiftieth anniversary of the liberation of Auschwitz in 1995 – it already provokes opposition. The discovery of the extent and ambition of the planned colonisation and change in land-tenure to be administered by the development of Auschwitz into a city seems to detract from the master-plan of the Final Solution, the plan to destroy the European Jews, which was carried out, and at Auschwitz, above all. Moreover, as I have tried to demonstrate, this approach also challenges the now-sacralised opposition between demonic reason and new ethics, between old Athens and New Jerusalem. According to that perspective, the new argument would normalise, or at least relativise, the evil which it explains. *And why should it not?* The answer would be:

34

because that shows no respect for those who died such terrible deaths, and, that it depends on discredited methods of knowledge, which also expired, as it were, in the gas-chambers. Against this, I discern in this refusal to 'relativise' a deeper fear: that we would then be part of that relativity *without there being any overarching law determining our participation*. And that would return us to a reflection on the boundaries of the city and the boundaries of the soul, which we would like to think we have overcome in the opposition between Athens and Jerusalem.

V

Let us return to the boundary wall of the city of Athens – here, just outside the boundary we find mourning women: Antigone, burying the body of her fratricidal brother in defiance of Creon's decree, witnessed by her reluctant sister, Ismene, who urges her to desist in the name of conformity to the law of the city; and the wife of Phocion, gathering the ashes of her disgraced husband, with her trusted woman companion, who, as the look-out, bears the political risk in her own contorted posture.

What is the meaning of these acts? Do they represent the transgression of the law of the city – women as the irony of the political community, as its ruination? Do they bring to representation an immediate ethical experience, 'women's experience', silenced and suppressed by the law of the city, and hence expelled outside its walls? No. In these delegitimate acts of tending the dead, these acts of justice, against the current will of the city, women reinvent the political life of the community.

By insisting on the right and rites of mourning, Antigone and the wife of Phocion carry out that intense work of the soul, that gradual rearrangement of its boundaries, which must occur when a loved one is lost – so as to let go, to allow the other fully to depart, and hence fully to be regained beyond sorrow. To acknowledge and to re-experience the justice and the injustice of the partner's life and death is to accept the law, it is not to transgress it – mourning becomes the law. Mourning draws on transcendent but representable justice, which makes the suffering of immediate experience visible and speakable. When completed, mourning returns the soul to the city, renewed and reinvigorated for participation, ready to take on the difficulties and injustices of the existing city. The mourner returns to negotiate and challenge the changing inner and outer boundaries of the soul and of the city; she returns to their perennial anxiety.

To oppose new ethics to the old city, Jerusalem to Athens, is to succumb to loss, to refuse to mourn, to cover persisting anxiety with the violence of a New Jerusalem masquerading as love. The possibility of structural analysis and of political action are equally undermined by the evasion of the anxiety and ambivalence inherent in power and knowledge. Why, I asked myself, did the large audience applaud so vigorously at the conference to celebrate the Centenary of Walter Benjamin's birth, held at University College London, last July, when told by a speaker that the masses have been anaesthetised by mass culture and mass media? What satisfaction, intellectual and political, is there in hearing the affirmation of total control? The active investment in power and anxious projection of it are exhibited in the response of that angry, anarchic audience to the proclamation of their own ineluctable disempowerment. This is to exhibit the same phantasised desire for political community without boundary walls at which to mourn; and without a soul, with its vulnerable and renegotiable boundaries, to bring to wail at those walls.

The hope of evading the risks of political community explains the appeal of one widespread version of the new ethics – the ethics of the other. The thought of the French Jewish philosopher, Emmanuel Levinas, has fast acquired the canonicity in modern philosophy that Maimonides has in medieval Jewish philosophy. His thinking, above all, has made Judaism available to the end of philosophy – philosophy which has discovered that it has no ethics, and which turns to Judaism as the sublime other of modernity. Levinas's *Buddhist* Judaism offers an extreme version of Athens versus Jerusalem. Knowledge, power and practical reason are attributed to the model of the autonomous, bounded, separated, individual self, the self within the city, 'the alliance of logic and politics'. The self, according to this new ethics, cannot experience truly transforming loss, but plunders the world for the booty of its self-seeking interest. To become ethical, this self is to be devastated, traumatised, unthroned, by the commandment to substitute *the other* for itself. Responsibility is defined in this new ethics as 'passivity beyond passivity', which is inconceivable and not representable, because it takes place beyond any city – even though Levinas insists that it is social and not sacred.

This new ethics denies identity to the other as it denies identity to the actor, now passive beyond passivity, more radically passive, that is, than any simple failure to act. But the other, too, is distraught and searching for political community – the other is also bounded and vulnerable, enraged and invested, isolated and interrelated. To command me to sacrifice myself in sublime passivity for the other, with no political expression for any activity, is to command in *ressentiment* an ethics of waving, whereas, as Stevie Smith put it in her poem *Not Waving but Drowning*.

> Nobody heard him the dead man
> But still he lay moaning
> I was much further out than you thought
> And not waving but drowning.

Stevie Smith drew a picture of him, too: with long, bedraggled tresses falling forward over his torso, erect above the indifferent waves. Without the soul and without the city, we cannot help anyone.

The presentation of this *Buddhist* Judaism as the sublime other of modernity, as the New Jerusalem, detracts from basic features of Judaism which are directly contrary to Levinas's thinking. First, rabbinic Judaism sees man as God's co-creator, not as creature, but as sublimely passive; secondly, prophetic Judaism stakes itself on transcendent justice that legitimates political activity, and does not place ethics beyond the world of being and politics; thirdly, rabbinic Judaism rests on the study of the law, *Talmud Torah*: it rests not on the devastation but on the *growth* of the self in knowledge. Learning in this sense mediates the social and the political: it works precisely by making mistakes, by taking the risk of action, and then by reflecting on its unintended consequences, and then taking the risk, yet again, of further action, and so on. Finally, far from being the sublime other of modernity, Judaism, in all its different modern forms, is immersed in the difficulties of modernity just as much as the philosophy, the sociology and the architectural history which have invested so much in its other-worldly beatification.

Elsewhere, I have tried to develop the idea and analysis of *the broken middle* in place of the opposition of Athens and Jerusalem (*The Broken Middle*, 1992). I try to develop the idea and analysis of *activity beyond activity*, to restate the risks of critical rationality and of political action, in place of this passivity beyond passivity. I do this by presenting the life, thought and politics of three German Jewish women within the political and social crises of their time: for the eighteenth century, Rahel Varnhagen; for the nineteenth and early twentieth century, Rosa Luxemburg; for the mid twentieth century, Hannah Arendt. In her own way, each of these women exposed the inequality and insufficiency of the universal political community of her day, but without retreating to any phantasy of the local or exclusive community: each staked the risks of identity without any security of identity.

Each suffered, struggled, acted and died at the boundary wall of *the third city*. Three modern women, for each of whom crossing the boundary wall into the city of Berlin was critical in her political and personal formation: I like to think of each of them entering the city, as Rahel Varnhagen had to, at the *Rosenthaler* gate, and of each returning to mourn and to be mourned at that same *Rosenthaler* gate – one of the three legal entry-points into the city for Jews in the eighteenth century.

Rosenthal means *valley of roses*; it is my name – the name that one branch of my family adopted in order to enter German civil society. So with this, I sign and conclude this lecture.

2

Beginnings of the day – Fascism and representation

I shall play the Fool to the *sovereignty* of the rubric 'Modernity, Culture and "the Jew"' hidden in its ethic of 'non-totalising' pluralism.

I shall start by questioning what I call 'Holocaust piety', evident across the whole range of responses to Spielberg's film *Schindler's List*, and I shall propose instead that we situate ourselves within what I call 'Holocaust ethnography'. 'Holocaust ethnography' permits the exploration of the representation of Fascism and the fascism of representation to be pursued across the production, distribution and reception of cultural works.

The demonstration that Fascism and representation are inseparable does not lead to the conclusion, current in post-modern aesthetics, philosophy and political theory, that representation is or should be superseded. On the contrary, the argument for the overcoming of representation, in its aesthetic, philosophical and political versions, converges with *the inner tendency* of Fascism itself.

Only the persistence of always fallible and contestable representation opens the possibility for our acknowledgement of mutual implication in the fascism of our cultural rites and rituals.

If Fascism promises beginnings of the day, representation exposes the interests of the middle of the day; then the owl of Minerva, flying at dusk, may reflect on the remains of the day – the ruins of the morning's hope, the actuality of the broken middles.

This chapter falls into three parts: Fascism and Aesthetic Representation; Fascism and Philosophical Representation; and Fascism and Political Representation.

FASCISM AND AESTHETIC REPRESENTATION

Schindler's List has been discussed ultimately in terms of its adequacy as memorial and monument to 'the Jews'. This involves a deeper argument than the generally agreed point that the film informs audiences, especially young audiences, of matters of which they would otherwise remain ignorant: that it overcomes knowledge-resistance to the Holocaust, a resistance which we know to be growing. Yet, as Freud argued, knowledge-resistance is the first and easiest of the five resistances to overcome. In particular, overcoming knowledge-resistance does not amount to working through the repressed emotions which dominate and inhibit the individual, so as to free the ego and restore effectivity.

At the heart of Bryan Cheyette's excellent review of *Schindler's List* (*TLS*, 18 February 1994), in which he compares the representation of the unequivocally sadistic Nazi, Goeth, with Schindler, 'a *tabula rasa* on which both the potential for good and evil can be inscribed', lies the following judgement: '*Schindler's List* fails only when it, too [like Keneally's original fictionalisation *Schindler's Ark*], becomes a seductive and self-confident narrative at the cost of any real understanding of the difficulties inherent *in representing the ineffable*' (my emphasis). Not surprisingly, one of the published critical replies to Cheyette (Alan G. Gross,

TLS, 18 March 1994) wholly rejects his nuanced appraisal of the film in the name of this 'ineffability', citing Habermas in support:

> There [in Auschwitz] something happened, that up to now nobody considered as even possible. There one touched on something which represents the deep layer of solidarity among all that wears a human face; notwithstanding the usual acts of beastliness of human history, the integrity of this common layer has been taken for granted . . . Auschwitz has changed the basis for the continuity of the conditions of life within history.

It is this reference to 'the ineffable' that I would dub 'Holocaust piety'. How is it to be construed and what is its economics? 'The ineffable' is invoked by a now wide-spread tradition of reflection on the Holocaust: by Adorno, by Holocaust theology, Christian and Jewish, more recently by Lyotard, and now by Habermas. According to this view, 'Auschwitz' or 'the Holocaust' are emblems for the breakdown in divine and/or human history. The uniqueness of this break delegitimises names and narratives as such, and hence all aesthetic or apprehensive representation (Lyotard).

The passage from Habermas indicates a trauma, a loss of trust in human solidarity, that marks the epoch which persists. In this way, the search for a decent response to those brutally destroyed is conflated with the quite different response called for in the face of the 'inhuman' capacity for such destruction. To argue for silence, prayer, the banishment equally of poetry and knowledge, in short, the witness of 'ineffability', that is, non-representability, is *to mystify something we dare not understand*, because we fear that it may be all too understandable, all too continuous with what we are – human, all too human.

What is it that we do not *want* to understand? What is it that Holocaust piety in film and reviews once again protects us from understanding?

In several places in his review, Bryan Cheyette compares Keneally's book unfavourably with the film. The book is said to 'glibly assimilate . . . an unimaginable past in a breathtakingly untroubled manner'. The film is judged to fail when it adopts an analogous filmic style, and to succeed when it has learnt from Primo Levi and from Claude Lanzmann's *Shoah*: the latter is said to be 'intellectually scrupulous and does not try to represent history in a facile series of cinematic tropes'. Elsewhere, Cheyette has argued that *Schindler's List* and *Shoah* are 'mirror images' of each other (*TLS*, 1 January 1994). I shall return to these comparisons with Levi and Lanzmann.

Keneally's book, I would argue, is not so *nice* about 'the ineffable'. The work is sceptical about the limitations of its own narrative, and, implicitly about the response of the reader. It opens with the dinner party at Commandant Goeth's attended by Schindler: 'Yet the revulsion Herr Schindler felt was of a piquant kind, an ancient exultant sense of abomination such as in a medieval painting, the just show for the damned. An emotion, that is, which stung Oskar rather than unmanned him' (p. 17). Oskar's, and, by implication, the reader's, participation *even in revulsion* in what is called 'the corrupt and savage scheme' of a capitalism dependent on slave labour, organised by a system of camps is, indeed, blithely, you could say 'glibly', emphasised. Any good which emerges from these presuppositions will be pragmatic and contingent; it will not be radical.

The book draws attention by litotes to further occasions for our 'ancient, exultant sense of abomination' when it describes the 'philosophic innocence' (p. 136) of Schindler in calling out 'one name', in saving one man (and, by implication, in saving 1,000) from the cattle wagon during the deportation that threatened to deprive him of his office manager, Abraham Bankier. The ruthlessness of saving one or 1,000, and in our exultant participating in that narrowly bounded victory, is *facetiously* contrasted with the Talmudic blessing, which is cited at the beginning of the book, not at the end, as in the film, that 'he who saves the life of one man saves the entire world' (p. 52). The book makes clear the pitiless immorality of this in the context: the film depends on it as congratulation.

In the book, political, cultural and religious differences within the formerly dispersed, so-called Jewish 'community' are reflected in the threatening character of the Jewish police, while the progressive brutalising of the Jews is manifest in the growing viciousness of the Jewish police to their people. The contagion of violence spares no one, whether the violence of collaboration or the violence of resistance; yet this is barely evident in the film.

The direct killing of individual children is eschewed in the film. Thus an episode from the book is excluded in which Schindler *is* 'unmanned'. During the liquidation of the ghetto, he watches the killing of a mother and son within the sight of the tiny, overwise girl in the red coat, who has also been rounded up. Schindler understands the indecency of exposing her to the shootings as the seal of her fate, too. He becomes acutely aware of the indecency of his own status as he stares down from a safe position. In the film, Schindler, a ludicrous saviour on a charger, dominates the liquidation from a promontory overlooking it. The audience is thereby spared the encounter with the indecency of their position.

The parallels between the family backgrounds of Amon Goeth and Oskar Schindler are brought out in the book. Both Austrian Catholics from undistinguished families, they are said to be each other's 'dark brother'. The comparison makes the reader's task harder in figuring out the reasons for the difference between what

Keneally cynically calls their 'reversible appetites', the difference in the individual outcome of their common origins.

Such plasticity of history, such pragmatics of good and evil, such continuity between *the banality of Schindler's benevolence* and the gratuity of Goeth's violence, should mean that the reader, and, *pari passu*, the audience, experience the crisis of identity in their own breasts. Instead, we enjoy vicarious revulsion at the handsome sadist, Goeth, who appears invincible in the film, but is imprisoned much earlier on in the book, and we applaud the *bonvivant* Schindler in his precarious outwitting of him.

However, it is the beginning and the end of book and film which diverge most profoundly. The book charts Schindler's 'progress' in the pragmatics of good and evil under the Talmudic irony of saving the entire world by saving one or 1,000 (the *Talmud* is ironic – the most ironic holy commentary in world literature: for no human being can save the world). At the end of the book, the presenting of the gold ring to Schindler, made from dental bridgework, which we saw earlier, in other circumstances, and knew to be extracted from the dead, marks 'the instant in which they [Schindler's Jews] become themselves again, [the instant] in which Oskar Schindler became dependent on gifts of theirs'. The book leads away from Talmudic irony: the film culminates in it and transforms it into brutal sincerity.

While the film informs us in a legend that Schindler's subsequent businesses and marriages failed, it does not make clear, as the 'Epilogue' to the book does, that Schindler thereafter never ceased to be the creature of his Jews. He travelled initially to Latin America with some of them, and was financed there in his various enterprises by them. And when he returned to Europe, he divided his time between penury in Frankfurt, relieved by his former Jews, and an annually celebrated mendicancy in Tel Aviv and Jerusalem, where he lived on the charity of his former Jews. This 'epilogue' brings out the master's dependence on his bondspeople *at every previous stage* in the story. The book, therefore, implies the incipient autonomy of the bondspeople; the film progressively mythologises hero, villain, survivors – the just and the damned.

After the scene of the excursion to Auschwitz, the film is degraded: the salvific waters which issue from the shower heads, as Bryan Cheyette points out, cause a crisis in the viewer who is suspended at the limit of the decency of witness. I would suggest that, from that point, there is no decent position: water not gas – to show the death agonies would exceed the limit of permissible representation; but water not gas induces the regressive identification ('philosophic innocence'?) with the few women who are saved. It is no coincidence that, from then, Schindler (whose visit to Auschwitz is only conjectural) becomes a demi-god, and the film degenerates into myth and sentimentality.

The sentimentality of the ultimate predator.

If the book is 'glib', it is because the story it tells is glib – the ironic, sustained glibness of the style is its integrity: it leaves the crisis to the reader.

The film depends on the sentimentality of the ultimate predator. It makes the crisis external: on first viewing, one is perpetually braced in fear of obscene excess of voyeuristic witness. This crisis is not the crisis of representation: it is the crisis of the sentimentality of the ultimate predator, whose complacency is left in place and wilfully reinforced by the last half hour of the film.

In a nature film, we could be made to identify with the life cycle of the fly as prey of the spider, and we could be made to identify with the life cycle of the spider as prey of the rodent. We can be made to identify with the Peking Opera singer who is destroyed by the Cultural Revolution, and we can equally be made to identify with the rickshaw man, for whom the Cultural Revolution was 'the beginning of Paradise'. It is only the ultimate predator whose sympathies can be so promiscuously enlisted. Only the ultimate predator who can be made to identify exclusively and yet consecutively with one link or another in the life cycle, because she can destroy the whole cycle, and, of course, herself. Since she is the ultimate predator, she can be sentimental about the victimhood of other predators while overlooking that victim's own violent predation; and she may embellish her arbitrary selectivity of compassion in rhapsodies and melodramas.

The limits of representation are not solely quantitative: how much violence, or even, what kind of violence, can I, and should I, tolerate? More profoundly, the limits of representation are configurative: they concern the relation between configuration and meaning.

It is my own violence that I discover in this film.

Schindler's List betrays the crisis of ambiguity in characterisation, mythologisation and identification, because of its anxiety that our sentimentality be left intact. It leaves us at *the beginning of the day*, in a Fascist security of our own unreflected predation, piously joining the survivors putting stones on Schindler's grave in Israel. It should leave us unsafe, but with *the remains of the day*. To have that experience, we would have to discover and confront our own fascism.

The comparison with Primo Levi's *If This is a Man* and Claude Lanzmann's *Shoah* will not help here. For the same limitations apply to the way in which they have been discussed. Bryan Cheyette contrasts *Schindler's List* with *Shoah* in two contrary ways: on the one hand, *Shoah* does not, like *Schindler's List*, represent every aspect of the apparatus of genocide with a 'facile series of cinematic tropes'; on the other hand, *Schindler's List* translates Lanzmann's *Shoah*, 'the best cinematic account [of the Holocaust] available' into his own rendering (op.cit.). Subsequently, Cheyette contrasts Lanzmann's 'modernist scepticism' with Spielberg's 'popular realism and sentimentalism' (*TLS*, 1 April 1994). Other discussions of *Shoah* use categories of 'witness' and 'testimony' uncritically in relation to the unknowable and inconceivable.[1]

However, *Shoah* raises questions of the interestedness of memory and recall on the part of the interviewer and the interviewed. While it does not rely on the filmic immediacy of fictionalised narrative, it depends on verbal narrations and representations which raise the same questions of the limit of representation. This is not the question of the limit of veracity, or of decency and obscenity in the representation of the past. It concerns the positioning of all categories of participants. The very form of question, respondent and historical referent, object of the agony of recall, imply a discrete object of attention, bounded, identified and located in the past. Yet it may be that the means of representation, *prima facie*, continuous with what they are interested in? This is to propose a critique of pure cinematic reason, where reason would examine its own nihilism, nihilism its own reason. Maybe only a film could explore this hermeneutic circle . . . I do not think that *Shoah* is 'sceptical': it is not self-referentially sceptical about its own means and form of representation.

The humane, temperate, restrained prose of Primo Levi's representation and witness did not protect or save him from the unexpressed ways in which he felt irrevocably contaminated by his experience, even though he knew that he had been effective in disseminating its witness. His notion of 'the grey zone' in *The Drowned and the Saved* comes nearest to capturing his sense of the collusion between executioner and victim. It can be compared with Tadeusz Borowski's account in the selection published under the title *This Way for the Gas, Ladies and Gentlemen* (1967). Borowski was a Pole but not a Jew, who killed himself in 1951. His account of being a prisoner in Auschwitz deals with many things which Levi spares us. Above all, Borowski represents himself, a deputy Kapo, as both executioner and victim, and deprives the distinction 'of all greatness and pathos'. While Borowski never denies his ethical presupposition – for otherwise not one sentence could have been written – he makes you witness brutality in the most disturbing way, for it is not clear – Levi always is – from what position, as whom, you are reading. You emerge shaking in horror at yourself, with yourself in question, not in admiration for the author's Olympian serenity (Levi).

Let us make a film in which the representation of Fascism would engage with the fascism of representation. A film, shall we say, which follows the life story of a member of the SS in all its pathos, so that we empathise with him, identify with his hopes and fears, disappointments and rage, so that when it comes to killing, we put our hands on the trigger with him, wanting him to get what he wants. We do this in all innocent enthusiasm in films where the vicarious enjoyment of violence may presuppose that the border between fantasy and reality is secure. Put starkly like this, this fantasy of a Nazi *Bildungsfilm* seems all too resistible, for the identity of the protagonist has been revealed in advance. If his future allegiances were not known, why should it not be possible to produce a dialectical lyric about such a character?

Compare, for example, Dina Wardi's important book *Memorial Candles: Children of the Holocaust* (Hebrew 1990, trans. 1992) with Joachim Fest's *The Face of the Third Reich* (German 1963, trans. 1970). Wardi reports on the psychology of children, most of whom were born to camp survivors in 1946. Fest explores the psychology of around twenty leading Nazis. Fest produces a political psychology of Nazism, while Wardi is concerned with the internalised psychic pathologies of children of camp survivors. Yet, the books tell the same story: that impotence and suffering arising from unmourned loss do not lead to a passion for objectivity and justice. They lead to resentment, hatred, inability to trust, and then, the doubled burden of fear of those negative emotions. This double burden is either turned inwards or outwards, but both directions involve denial. It is the abused who become the abusers, whether politically as well as psychically may depend on contingencies of social and political history.

We have seen the film, read the book, which represents this story: a film about violence in which not one blow is cast, a deeply erotic film in which not even a wrist is visible: the Merchant-Ivory film *Remains of the Day*, based on the novel of the same title by Kazuo Ishiguro. This film explores the ethics of the dedicated service of the head butler – the servant, the bondsman – to a Lord, who tries, from 1923, to lead the British political class to support the Nazi movement, and then the Hitler government. While the story concerns the British class structure, it depicts the attractions of, and arguments for, supporting the Nazi cause to the Lord, and it examines the collusion of the servant in his master's politics.

The servant finds himself in the contradiction of the ethic of service. The career of true service is not solely domestic excellence, but advancement to the employ of the noblest Lord, the morally humanitarian Lord, the Lord who himself most serves the general good. However, once the pledge of service has been vowed to the Lord thus elected, it is staked on disinterested, unquestioning commitment. This commitment presupposes the inviolable integrity of the Lord's relation to his counterparts, the international confraternity of diplomatic and governing classes, still drawn in Europe in the 1920s and 30s from the old aristocracies.

The film shows that the dilemma of this inspired and blinkered service, the idealism of which permits a lifetime of total restraint and discipline, arises out of and issues in a personality which is loveless, and which wards off and refuses love. The incapacity of the British upper classes and their servants to impart the facts of life to the next generation (Lord Darlington asks Stevens to communicate these matters to his god-son) is palpably linked to their common inability to express and work through emotion.

The film is almost unbearably moving because it breaks the barrier of passive sobriety or sentimentality of witness, and induces active recognition in oneself of the nihilism of disowned emotions, and the personal and political depredations at stake. To achieve this kind of representation, the film centres on the drama of the relation between the butler, Stevens, and the housekeeper, Miss Kenton. In the book, the political framework and the butler's story are more evenly balanced.

The attractions of German Nazism are present in microcosm in the organization of the aristocratic household as a fascist corporation. The members of that corporation are *free* in their initial pledge of loyalty, but become *unfree* in their consequent total rescinding of the right to criticise. They have espoused the ideal of *dignity* as unstinting service to the noble Lord, and have rejected the idea of *dignity* as the liberal, representative notion of citizenship, or as the struggles of socialism. These contrasting ideals of dignity emerge clearly towards the end of the story in the discussion in the pub to which Stevens is involuntarily drawn. In the book, the analogies between the structure and incapacities of the soul of the servant and those of the household and the state are equally foregrounded. In the film, the loveless upbringing of the servant, confessed by his father on his deathbed, is substituted for his *unexplained* conviction of having inherited the benign but exacting notion of selfless service from his father in the book.

Now, of course, this is not a representation of mobilised Fascism, which breaks the barrier between the fantasy of revenge and the carrying out of murderous feelings on arbitrarily selected scapegoats by joining a movement which has publicly abolished the distinction between fantasy and political action.

The servant bears the burden of his passions: the idea of dignity as restraint, avoidance of 'unseeming demonstrativeness' – the notion of corporate dignity which threatens to rob him of all liberal dignity – leads him equally to make 'mistakes' in his professional, political and personal life. He bears this burden in a heart which distends to breaking point in his meeting with Miss Kenton, married for many years, when he, once again, restrains himself even in the face of her quasi-confession of undying passion. This moment of controlled but excruciating pain in film and book is *not his salvation*. But it gives him *the remains of the day* – 'dignity' minimally reassembled out of the ruins of ideals, out of pieces of broken heart ('the remains'). In the book, the servant resolves to aspire to the idea of human warmth: to be practised by cultivating a bantering, ironic form of civility – the liberal tempering of his former unrelieved servility – towards his new American 'Lord' ('the day').

This film dramatises the link between emotional and political collusion. Without sentimental voyeurism, it induces a crisis of identification in the viewer, who is brought up flat against equally *the representation of Fascism*, the *honourable* tradition which could not recognise the evils of Nazism, and the corporate order of the great house, and *the fascism of representation*, a political culture which we identify as our own, and hence an emotional economy which we cannot project and disown.

The ultimate predator is not suspended in a saddle on a charger, overlooking from a promontory, with a piquant revulsion, with the ancient, exultant sense of abomination, such as, in a medieval painting the just show for the damned, or joining the queue of survivors. Instead of emerging with sentimental tears, which leave us emotionally and politically intact, we emerge with the dry eyes of a deep grief, which belongs to the recognition of our ineluctable grounding in the norms of the emotional and political culture represented, and which leaves us with the uncertainty of the remains of the day.

FASCISM AND PHILOSOPHICAL REPRESENTATION

The *representation of Fascism* leaves the identity of the voyeur intact, at a remove from the grievous events which she observes. Her self-defences remain untouched, while she may feel *exultant revulsion* or *infinite pity* for those whose fate is displayed. She experiences those *medieval passions* which do not 'unman' her. But we are not medievals, we are *moderns*: our moral will defends our particular interests, while we try to eschew those experiences which expose the common threshold of the will with both our vulnerable singularity and our hesitant universality.

The *fascism of representation*, beyond the limit of voyeurism, provokes the grief of encountering the violence normally legitimised by the individual moral will, with which we defend our own particular interests, and see only the egoism of the other – these may be interests of disinterested service, race, gender, religion, class. This grief expresses the crisis of the dissolution of particular identity and the vision of the universal. Across the unprotected exposure of our singularity, of our otherness to ourselves, we sense the 'we', which we otherwise so partially and carelessly assume.

This range of response, the representation of Fascism and the fascism of representation, is inherent in the media of representation.

Philosophy would abolish representation. The translation of modern metaphysics into ontology involves, first and last, the overcoming of representation as the *imperium* of the modern philosophical subject, and as the false promise of universal politics. Heideggerian and post-Heideggerian ontology seeks to replace the hubris of the metaphysical subject, which, in its abstract self-relation represents itself to itself, or, as the will, actualises itself, *infinitely* in any object, by an ontology of *finite* beings. The giving of Being to beings, who live and die, contrasts with the subject of representation, abstracted from the finitude and vicissitudes of *existence*. Ontology claims to open up themes to which the self-confident subject of philosophy is impervious: the abyss, anxiety, care.

According to ontology, the discourse of individual rights depends on this metaphysics of the subject, for the idea of universal human and civil rights is founded on the assumption of individuals present to themselves, and therefore to others, as self-relating, so that difference is only the moment overcome in the assertion of abstract identity. This notion of political representation is said to have its failure built into it. For what can be acknowledged is only the other as self-related in identity, or only difference within self-relation, but not difference *proper*.

In one recent version of ontology, evil is understood as *radical* (see Jean-Luc Nancy, *The Experience of Freedom*, trans. 1993). This flies in the face of the tradition of neo-platonic Christianity, according to which evil is merely the deprivation of good (*privatio boni*), and has no independent reality. According to this tradition, only good is radical. Hence Hannah Arendt's analysis of Eichmann in terms of 'the banality of evil' implies a reassertion of the tradition of the radicality of the good. (What I have called 'the banality of Schindler's benevolence' amounts to an ironic comment on that tradition.) In the new ontology, evil is the insistence in the face of existential groundlessness on a foundation, the refusal of the abyss. (This argument seems to me to be a typical *privatio boni* argument.) Insistence on ground is said to be the process involved in the Nazi myth of racial superiority.

However, this 'positivity of evil' in its generality becomes indistinguishable from what would be *the evil of any positing*. Hegel's *labour* of spirit, which tarries with the negative, knows its freedom only in destruction, and 'secures its self-presence in recollection', is made indistinguishable from evil, once evil is defined as the flight from groundlessness. The *positivity of evil* cannot be distinguished from *the evil of the positive*, since there is no way of distinguishing between flight from ground into the *fixity* of self and other identity, and an initial self-identity which discovers itself to be *fluid* not fixed, which encounters the violence towards the other in its initial self-definition, and undergoes transformations of the initial identity. Ontology can only read experience as identitarian. 'The life of spirit is not one that shuns death, and keeps clear of destruction; it endures death and in death maintains its being.' Ontology sees only the obscene colonising of death in this; for it cannot admit that the subject has any actual experience: that in its posited particularity it may be constantly exposed to *the aporia* – not the self-identity – of its particularity with the singularity and the universality of itself and others.

In its desire to escape the murderous complacencies imputed to representation, ontology, however, falls into paradoxes of its own invention. It must employ the resources of language, that is, the premises of representation, in its attempt to speak ontologically. This accounts for the linguistic licence associated with ontology and its offshoots, post-structuralism and post-modernism. It also produces the crisis of post-ontology, 'beyond Being', as the discourse of Being itself inevitably comes to be perceived as yet another objectification of Being, as self-identical or positive, and hence as partaking in the positivity of evil. Heidegger's Nazism becomes evidence of this insufficient radicalising of the metaphysical tradition, which is intrinsic to the medium of radicalisation itself. The result of these self-perpetuating inversions is that the question whether the ontological relinquishing of representation displays *the same impulse* as the politics it espoused cannot be pursued. (The Jews, after all, were destroyed not for their pretensions as political subjects, but for their sheer existence, their belonging to Being.)

Post-modern ontology misrepresents the development of modern philosophy. For philosophy has *abolished itself in two quite different ways* in response to the claim of the moral autonomy of the philosophical subject. It has *aestheticised* itself in the ontological replacement of critical philosophy, which finds its way to Being via the aesthetics of the sublime. And it has *politicised* itself. By this I do not mean the scientific or utopian method of socialism. I do not mean to set out once again the apparent opposition between nihilism and rationalism.

I mean to draw attention to a construal (which I could call Hegel *or* Nietzsche) which has expounded the autonomous moral subject as free within the order of representations and unfree within its preconditions and outcomes, and modernity as the working out of that combination. Ontology asserts the contrary: that the subject is unfree within representation, and, understood as *Dasein*, 'free' beyond its presuppositions and outcomes. In the approach which I contrast to ontology, the nihilism of power is related to the positivity of legal and rational authority by a methodology which is *alive to its implication in both nihilism and reason*, and which *does not know the outcome in advance*. The sovereign subject is not dethroned in the name of the ineffable singularity of Being, but released for the perilous adventures in the always precarious configurations of rationalised domination. In these adventures, the moral will guarding its particular interests is confronted by the excess which it comes to know as its singularity and universality.

If fascism is the triumph of civil society, the triumph of enraged particular interests, then the subject of representation does not need to be superseded: the danger of its experience needs to be exposed. And the same danger will be the means of exposition.

Otherwise we remain at a beginning of the day.

FASCISM AND POLITICAL REPRESENTATION

In the course of three years we have moved from Francis Fukuyama's congratulatory and despairing *End of History and the Last Man* (1992) to the despair of Edward Luttwak's 'Fascism is the Wave of the Future' (*LRB*, 7 April 1994). The revolt of 'the last man' provides the fatal connection.

The resurgence of Fascism in political bodies with a tradition of liberal constitutional government (Italy) needs to be distinguished from its development in those without such a tradition (Russia, where the Party was the ruler of the USSR). Speculation concerning the proclivity to Fascism in a political body with no history of Fascism (Luttwak speculates about the United States in these terms), needs to be distinguished from its renaissance in political bodies which have a history of Fascism.

It is important to distinguish between fascist movements, fascist seizures of power, fascist governments, and the general thesis that the post-Second World War world has assimilated fascist characteristics into state and society. Whereas in the thirties, fascist movements seized power, what we may be witnessing now is the transition from endemic fascism to the new seizure of power.

If fascist movements and the fascist seizure of power imply the leadership principle, mass mobilisation, mix of legality and terror, then the so-called 'Fascist state' implies, in addition, abolition of political parties, rights, representation and voluntary associations, the corporate state, legal-irrational bureaucracy, mix of policing by rule of law and by terror, nationalism and racism. 'Endemic' fascism has been analysed in terms of 'the culture industry', 'the administered world', and the continuities of everyday life in Germany from the 1930s to 1950s – all dramatic overstatements, designed to defamiliarise modern familiarities.

The representation of Fascism and the fascism of representation presupposes the definition of the modern, liberal state as *the monopoly of the means of legitimate violence*; it is thus able to explore the changing configurations of violence and legality on which fascism in all its modes relies. This is not therefore to advance the new teleology of Auschwitz, that all rationalisation is violence. Here, the inquiring voice presupposes its own implication in the stakes of reason and power, and does not know the outcome in advance.

The thesis of the 'individualization of social inequality' has been developed by Ulrich Beck as characteristic of what he calls 'the risk society' (*Risk Society: Towards a New Modernity*, trans. 1992). In this society, risks that were formerly absorbed by classes and by families are now borne by individuals, whose lives do not unfold within, and are not protected by, those traditional categories. As a sociological thesis, this is to offer a description of political ideology as the explanation of social structural change. However, the social consequences of the political *conceptualisation* of individuals as tax-payers and consumers, and not as workers are critical. As workers, we are all, in fact, increasingly subject to insecurity of employment across the occupational structure, to worsening, systematic, class inequality, which, however, we do not understand or express in terms of traditional class identities and allegiances.

Libertarian ideology masks the concentration of the monopoly of legitimate violence in the centralised state, which, formerly, was effectively delegated and dispersed across the quasi-independent institutions of the middle. And it masks *the unleashing of the non-legitimate violence of individualised civil society*, which is provoked by the systematic inequality arising from that concentration. Fascist movements seek the *monopoly of non-legitimate violence*: that is why they require the rule of law, which they also undermine. They seek to overturn the age-old impulse and wisdom of politics: that to guarantee my self-preservation and the protection of my initially usurped property, I must grant the same guarantees to the persons and property of others. Fascist movements want universal law to apply so that they may have no rivals in their use of non-legitimate violence. They represent the triumph of civil society, the realm of individual need, the war of particular interests. They exploit the already partisan mediation of the instrumentalised universal – the epitome of what Hegel called 'the spiritual-animal kingdom'. This is how it is possible to anticipate that states which combine social libertarianism with political authoritarianism, whether they have traditional class parties or not, could become susceptible to fascist movements.

The representation of Fascism and the fascism of representation contrasts equally with classic and revisionist Marxism, and with Orientalism, the politics of identity.

Marxist theory implies that political practice follows from the analysis of class structure and class interests. This does not mean the derivation of 'ought' from 'is', but that the universal interest is generated in the dynamic of capitalist development itself. There is, nevertheless, room for action, because if theory and practice are inseparable, they also strain towards each other, as classes-in-themselves become classes-for-themselves in the circumstances of crises of overproduction. The proletariat is represented as the potentially universal class, the class which may genuinely claim that its particular interests correspond to the universal interest. The question 'What ought I to do?' is valid within the mesh of theory and practice. Some of my students still pose it: whatever the particular class position of the individual, they yearn to find the mode of effective political action which will *necessarily* further the universal interest.

The representation of Fascism and the fascism of representation invalidates this approach. Marxism tends to assume that the intellectual, individual or class is somehow innocent of political practice until the theoretical work is accomplished, and the relation between particular and universal interest clarified. According to the representation of Fascism and the fascism of representation, the will to power is already engaged as a political will. We are already politically active, whether or not we embrace programme, party or movement. We are always staking ourselves in the representation of Fascism and the fascism of representation throughout the range of quotidian practices and cultural rituals – when we go to the cinema, for instance.

This differs equally from Orientalism or the politics of identity.

The representation of Fascism and the fascism of representation does not work with the opposition between the agent of imperial domination and the oppressed other. It points out that 'the other' is also agent, enraged and invested; while the idea of the monolithic, imperialist agent amounts to the consolidation and reification of power, the dilemma of which is thereby disowned. The representation of Fascism and the fascism of representation does not oppose the idea of totalising power to the degrading of its others, nor does it propose cultural pluralism as its expiation. It understands all agents *in power and out of it* to face the dilemma of asserting their moral will solely to guard their particular interests.

For politics does not happen when you act on behalf of your own damaged good, but when you act, *without guarantees*, for the good of all – this is to take *the risk* of the *universal* interest. Politics in this sense requires representation, the critique of representation, and the critique of the critique of representation.

Thus I play the Fool to the sovereignty of the rubric which assembles us: 'Modernity, Culture and "the Jew"' with its freighted and fraught agglomeration of terms.

Yet we have had trust enough to tarry.

Now, dare I hope: it is slightly later in the day.

3

The comedy of Hegel and the *Trauerspiel* of modern philosophy

The general ground for comedy is therefore a world in which man as subject or person has made himself completely master of everything that counts to him otherwise than the essential content of what he wills and accomplishes, a world whose purposes are therefore destroyed because of their unsubstantiality. Nothing can be done, for example, to help a democratic nation where the citizens are self-seeking, quarrelsome, frivolous, bumptious, without faith or knowledge, garrulous, boastful and ineffectual: such a nation destroys itself by its own folly.

Hegel is keen to distinguish the merely *laughable* from *the comical* in the sequel to this passage from page 1,199 of the English translation of his *Aesthetics*.[1] We may laugh at any contrast between subjective caprice and insubstantial action, while vice and evil are not in themselves comic: 'There is also the laughter of derision, scorn, despair, etc. On the other hand, the comical as such implies an infinite light-heartedness and confidence felt by someone raised altogether above his own inner contradiction and not bitter or miserable in it at all; this is the bliss and ease of a man who, being sure of himself, can bear the frustrations of his aims and achievements' (p. 1,200). (Is this condition of serenity, I wonder, attained by effort or by grace?) In comedy, 'the ruling principle is the contingency and caprice of subjective life' whose nullity and self-destructive folly displays the abused actuality of substantial life (pp. 1,1800, 1,202). The aberration of the passions that rage in the human heart are drawn from 'the aberrations of the democracy out of which the old faith and morals have vanished' (as Hegel describes Aristophanes' comedies) (p. 1,163). While in tragedy the powers which oppose each other as pathos in individuals are hostile, in comedy, 'they are revealed directly as inwardly self-dissolving' (p. 1,163). Comedy, as much as tragedy, is always *divine comedy*: 'the Divine here in its community, as the substance and aim of human individuality, brought into existence as something concrete, summoned into action and put in movement' (p. 1,162).

In the work of mourning and the search for *the new ethics*, in which philosophy is currently engaged in the wake of the perceived demise of Marxism and, equally, of the disgrace of Heidegger's Nazism, the comedy of Hegel (by which I mean *not* what Hegel says about comedy but *the movement of the Absolute as comedy*) is, nevertheless, once again being ignored and maligned by the neo-nihilism and antinomianism which continue – but at increasingly crippling cost – to evade their inner self-perficient impulse.[2] As a result, mourning *cannot work*: it remains melancholia;[3] it remains *aberrated* not *inaugurated*;[4] pathos of the concept in the place of its logos. Instead of producing a work, this self-inhibited mourning produces a play, the *Trauerspiel*, the interminable mourning play and lament, of post-modernity.

The urgency and currency of this search for a *new ethics* – for an ethics, that is, without grounds, principle, transcendence or utopia – should not be allowed to obscure the way in which the fate of modern philosophy is hereby repeated. For, since Kant, philosophy has nurtured its unease with the modern diremption of law and ethics, arising from the mismatch between the discourse of individual rights and the systematic actualities of power and domination, by fixating on external statements of Hegel's argument with Kant and of Marx's argument with Hegel. Philosophy since Kant has never achieved a freely mobile and genuinely critical relationship to Hegel's thinking, nor, *a fortiori*, to the inversions structuring modern subjectivity and ethical substance in which it embroils itself more blindly and deeply with the totalising invocation of metaphysics overcome.

In a lecture which he delivered recently at the University of Warwick (April 1993) entitled 'Spectres of Marx: the State of the Debt, the Work of Mourning and the New International',[5] Derrida set out to complete the work of mourning for Marxism: what he accomplishes, however, is *the aberration of mourning* for the spirit, the spectre, of Heidegger. Taking as his text the first paragraph of Marx's *Communist Manifesto*:

> A spectre is haunting Europe – the spectre of Communism. All the powers of old Europe have entered into a holy alliance to exorcise this spectre: Pope and Czar, Metternich and Guizot, French Radicals and German police-spies.

Derrida turns the metaphor of 'the spectre' of Communism into licence for the idea and operation of what he names 'the spirit of Marxism': the ghost of Communism will finally be laid to rest if this spirit – dare one say this *essence*? – of Marxism is retrieved from the rubble of old Europe, before the fresh rubble, accruing daily in a new Europe that is dying not to be born, submerges us all.

What is the shape of this spirit? Could it be the spirit of Marxism *as a method*, which Lukacs reclaimed from Marxism as dogma in his foundational essay from 1919, 'What is Orthodox Marxism?'[6] On the contrary! Opposed to any such archi-teleological and pneumatological notion of spirit, Derrida's use of the discourse and metaphor of spirit captures the *heterogeneous-originary* spirit, which, he has argued elsewhere, Heidegger developed by way of otherwise mute expiation for his lapse into the metaphysics of spirit and 'subjectity' (*sic*) in the *Rectoral Address*.[7]

In distancing himself from Althusser's legacy, what does Derrida assert is discardable as the body of Marxism, and why? Class structure, class consciousness and class struggle, the party, the laws of capitalist accumulation, the theory of value, human practical activity. In effect, each and every component of Marx's theory as it strains towards practice is said to be an index of bourgeois culture: dialectical materialism, the iron laws of necessity, present mirror-images of the rigidities of logocentrism; and they were realised not in proletarian revolution but in the fate of the modern state – in Stalinism, in Fascism and in Nazism.

The body of Marxism arrayed in its shroud may finally rest in peace, for its vital spirit, its anima, has been thoroughly etherealised and floats in a heaven of archi-original Messianic justice. But wait! – the resurrection of the dead *in their flesh* was a dogma developed for the Hebrews, who could not conceive in Hebrew of the immortality of the Greek soul – *psyche* – separated from the Greek body – *soma*. Language to the Hebrews was physical: the idea of an eternity without body not bliss but unimaginable torture. Let us therefore tarry with those bleached bones; for as we seek to pay them their last respects, they seem to be rearranging themselves in an articulate and urgent configuration.

Derrida's strongest argument for construing Marx's *Capital* as the exposition of 'spirit' draws on the analysis of 'the mystical character of the commodity', the theory of commodity fetishism. The famous statement of this occurs in the first chapter of the first volume of *Capital*. Marx says that 'in order to find an analogy' for the way exchange value transforms 'the social connections between persons . . . into a social relation between things'

> we must have recourse to the most-enveloped regions of the religious. In that world the productions of the human brain appear as independent beings endowed with life, and entering into relation both with one another and the human race

'So it is in the world of commodities . . . A definite social relation between people assumes the phantasmagoric form of a relation between things.'[8] Derrida extends the phantasmagoric illusion which Marx argues arises from 'exchange value' (the way in which the value of a commodity when exchanged seems to be as 'natural' or inherent in it as any of its other physical properties or uses) to 'use-value' itself. Quite rightly, he points out that the logic of the idea of 'use-value' (the value of a thing in use) is incoherent if it is posited as the originary moment prior to the operation of capital. However, once use value is also conceived as 'phantasmagoric', then the world of capital circulates among the crowds of dim and doubtfully real persons, who are equally insubstantial whether they stand for wage-labour or the personification of the commodity.

Derrida has forgotten Marx's materialism and Hegel's *Logic*, on which Marx's account of commodity fetishism depends. Without positing a suprasystemic origin, Marx expounds the inequality between those who sell their labour-power as a thing, as a commodity, and those who own the means of production. It is this discrepancy between the formal equality of the wage-contract (and equally of the form of money) and the substantial inequality of the parties to the contract that initiates the exposition of the capital/wage-labour relationship. The theory of commodity fetishism serves to explain the way this dynamic inequality generates further social and political forms which systematically obscure the structure and workings of the relationship. Marx's exposition draws on Hegel's logic of illusion, according to which relations between apparently independent determinations can be seen as internally generated relations. This is the measure of Marx's materialism; it is what he means by 'a definite social relation'.

There is no materialism in Derrida's account of Marx. The messianism of Derrida's call for the New International emerges as the correlate of this missing impetus. The New International has no body: so how can it have any members? It has no law, no community, no institutions. This spectral idea of internationalism represents the most explicit emergence of the anarchic utopianism at the heart of postmodern thinking: it is the very antithesis of Marx's 'scientific socialism', but it is this antithesis because it projects a science of laws, a determinism, onto Marx's thought which seems utterly ignorant of the debt to Hegel in Marx's method.

In the 'note' to *De l'esprit*, Derrida reduces (in the Husserlian sense of *epoché*, the transcendental bracketing of the whole world, including ourselves and our thinking) Heidegger's imputed heterogeneous origin to the event of promise, the promise of promises, archi-promise, prior, he claims, to 'all the testaments, all the promises, all the events, all the laws and assignments which are our very memory'.[9] This reduction is said to radicalise the Heideggerian *question* with its residual overtone of Enlightenment rationality. Indeed it does: for what is prior to memory, law, event, assignment, but the covenant between God and His chosen people – the Hebrews – which is the origin both of their sacred and of their historical relationship? And what is promised – the promise of promises, originary *and* deferred – but the Messiah? This Messianic spirit of Marxism has been reborn into *a holy family*: it is the offspring of the Heideggerian origin reduced to archi-promise and of deconstruction defined as justice in terms borrowed – with equal trepidation on Derrida's part as evinced in his Heideggerian borrowing – from Walter Benjamin's Messianic political theology of divine and law-founding violence.[10]

Derrida adopts Benjamin's idea of divine law-abolishing violence and develops the claim that deconstruction is the origin, in effect, the measure, of ungroundable justice,[11] from Benjamin's last great *Trauerspiel* or mourning play: the thirty-six 'Theses on the Philosophy of History'.[12] The essay by Benjamin, 'Critique of Violence', which Derrida deconstructs to its originary, divine, law-abolishing violence,[13] anticipates the philosophy of law developed in Benjamin's greatest work, *The Origin of German Trauerspiel*.[14] This philosophy of law – of all human and positive law as fallen, violent and unredeemable – leads seamlessly from Benjamin's exposition of Counter-Reformation mourning plays, of baroque Christianity, both Catholic and Protestant, in this early work, to the Judaic Messianism of the final theses, in which all the features of baroque *Trauerspiel* are attributed to the failure of Social Democracy to oppose Fascism – 'the enemy has not ceased to be victorious' – by *a counter-state of emergency*, which would suspend all law and history as it erupts: total, bloodless violence is to assuage and redeem all the partial and bloody violence of history. These are Benjamin's terms combusted to an eschatological originary on Derrida's ignition.

This is no work of mourning: it remains baroque melancholia immersed in the world of soulless and unredeemed bodies, which affords a vision that is far more disturbing than the salvific distillation of disembodied 'spirit' or 'spectre'. For if all human law is sheer violence, if there is no positive or symbolic law to be acknowledged – the law that decrees the absence of the other, the necessity of relinquishing the dead one, returning from devastating inner grief to the law of the everyday and of relationships, old and new, with those who live – then there can be *no work*, no exploring of the legacy of ambivalence, working through the contradictory emotions aroused by bereavement. Instead, the remains of the dead one will be incorporated into the soul of the one who cannot mourn and will manifest themselves in some all too physical symptom, the allegory of incomplete mourning in its desolate hyper-reality.

This is *aberrated*, not *inaugurated* mourning: it suits the case of Heidegger, who never mourned, who never spoke about his Nazism or about the Nazi genocide of six million Jews. However, where Marxism is concerned, far from rescuing some quintessential 'spirit', this approach reduces Marxism (in the ordinary sense of diminution, not in the philosophical sense of abstention) to a sub-rational pseudo-Messianism, while disqualifying both critical reflection and political practice. It is a counsel of hopelessness which extols Messianic hope.

All this stems from the *logophobic* ethos of Derrida's thinking (pardon my neologism). Desperate for expiation and for ethics, he nevertheless desires to avoid *at all costs* renewing the question (yes, the *question*), which Marx himself posed and from which his thinking, young and old, proceeded: 'How do we stand in relation to the Hegelian dialectic?'[15] Only our taking on the burden of posing this question anew would permit us to investigate the possibility of an ethics which does not remain naive and ignorant of its historical and political presuppositions and hence of its likely outcomes. Such an ethics requires a comprehensive account of substance and subject, of modernity and subjectivity; an account, that is, of the modern fate of ethical life: of the institutional and individual inversions of meaning in the modern state and society, where increase in subjective freedom is accompanied by decrease in objective freedom, where the discourses of individual rights distract from the actualities of power and domination.

Once the question of the relation to the Hegelian dialectic has been posed anew for our time, two responses to this question need to be distinguished: *the one that I have been developing so far*, which has discerned the relation to the Hegelian dialectic on the part of a post-modern consciousness that restricts its operation to *the dialectical oppositions of the Understanding*, and proceeds dualistically and deconstructively; and the one that I have also been insinuating, which comprehends the dualisms and deconstructions of the first response as the dynamic movement of a political history which can be expounded speculatively out of the broken middle. The response encountered so far is tragic in the sense of the baroque mourning play, *aberrated* mourning; the response to be developed further here will be comic – the comedy of absolute spirit, *inaugurated* mourning.

Let us contine to chase spirits back into their bodies, back into the history of their development, in order to comprehend their law and their anarchy and to complete the work of mourning. Reincarnated, put back into their bodies, as it were, 'spectres' in Marx, 'ghosts' in Heidegger, join up with class conflict in the former and with heterogeneous-originary iterable violence in the latter which deconstruction owns as its primordial and hence undeconstructable justice.

'Spirit' in Hegel's *Phenomenology of Spirit* never leaves its body. Yet the response to Hegel's dialectic which is characteristic of dualistic and deconstructive Understanding purveys *three massive misunderstandings* concerning 'spirit' in Hegel: first, 'spirit' is understood to mean 'breath' (*pneuma*) in opposition to matter, and to be teleological and final; secondly, this ascendancy of 'spirit' over its other, 'matter', indicates the ruse of *reason*, or, rather, its sheer bloody-mindedness in its general privilege over, and suppression of, all its Others; third, *law* in the *Phenomenology* is imperial, with the moment of *The Antigone* providing the excess which breaks out of the *Phenomenology* – woman breaching both the closed circuit of the patriarchal community and of Hegel's watertight system.

Well, what a comedy of caricatures and errors! And I, in turn, must join this comedy of type-casting in order to insinuate *the absolute comedy*: for I must represent and hence misrepresent to you the modality and meaning of the *Phenomenology* – its 'spirit' as much as its grievous fate.

Let me then shoot from a pistol: first, *spirit* in the *Phenomenology* means *the drama of misrecognition* which ensues at every stage and transition of the work – a ceaseless comedy, according to which our aims and outcomes constantly mismatch each other, and provoke yet another revised aim, action and discordant outcome. Secondly, *reason*, therefore, is comic, full of surprises, of unanticipated happenings, so that comprehension is always provisional and preliminary. This is the meaning of *Bildung*, of formation or education, which is intrinsic to the phenomenological process. Thirdly, *the law* is no longer that of Greek ethical life; it is no longer tragic. Antigone stakes her life as the individuated pathos of substantial life in collision with itself: she presents part of its truth and she acknowledges the part of that truth *which exceeds her*. By contrast, modern law is that of *legal status*, where those with subjective rights and subjective ends deceive themselves and others that they act for the universal when they care only for their own interests. This is *the spiritual-animal kingdom*: it is comic, not in the sense of frank joviality or careless gaiety and self-mockery, but in the sense of bitter and repugnant intrigue by individuals who deceive others by seeming to share their interests and whose real interest is without substance. These modern comic characters are unmasked by others and not by their own self-dissolving inwardness of humour.[16]

Now all this requires detailed exposition: I could show how the struggle for recognition between lord and bondsman issues in the education of the bondsman through his experience of fear both of the absolute master – death – and of the relative master – the lord. The bondsman is able to overcome both kinds of fear by risking his life and by working, by acknowledging the plasticity of the world and hence the otherness of the lord, of matter, of himself, while the lord only discovers his dependence on the bondsman. The outcome of this is not, however, the triumph of the bondsman (nor the working class in its relation to the bourgeoisie, as has been erroneously extrapolated to Marx) but *the internalisation of the struggle* between lord and bondsman in *the status of the legal person*. Individuals, defined abstractly as legal persons, lose their relation to desire, work and otherness, their own and that of others. Legal persons understand themselves to be confronting 'the world' in unstable attempts to maintain a stoical or sceptical relation to it, when 'the world' has itself been compacted and projected out of the misrecognition of work, desire and engaged otherness. This alienation of 'the world' and subsequent abjection of the self result in the unhappy consciousness.

The *Phenomenology* continues to explore the misadventures of the self-consciousness of the legal person in its various misunder-standings of otherness as *the world*: 'Virtue and the way of the world', 'the spiritual-animal kingdom and deceit'. These are some of Hegel's comic sub-sectional titles, which introduce phenome-nological explorations of the hypertrophy of subjective life con-comitant with modern, individual freedom of rights, on the migration of ethical substance (objective freedom) into the hapless subject.

Now in presenting phenomenology schematically and topically like this, I am, of course, giving you *the results*, not the experience, process or *Bildung* of self-consciousness as it comes up against, again and again, its own positing of 'the world', discovering out-comes the inverse of what it intended. Seeking pleasure, for example, self-consciousness encounters necessity, 'the grave of life'. And I wish to conclude on the terrain of *results* by drawing out three which support my argument that *inaugurated* mourning requires the relation to law that is presented by *the comedy of absolute spirit* as found in Hegel's *Phenomenology*.

First, then, far from absorbing otherness back into self-con-sciousness or subjectivity (Fichte's position which Hegel designed the *Phenomenology* to oppose), the presentation of otherness has a motility which the post-modern gesture towards otherness is unable to conceive. For the separation out of otherness as such is derived from the failure of mutual recognition on the part of two self-consciousnesses who encounter each other and refuse to recognise the other as itself a self-relation: the other is never simply other, but an implicated self-relation. This applies to oneself as other and, equally, to any opposing self-consciousness: my relation to myself is mediated by what I recognise or refuse to recognise in your relation to yourself; while your self-relation depends on what you recognise of my relation to myself. *We are both equally enraged and invested*, and to fix our relation in domination or dependence is unstable and reversible, to fix it as 'the world' is to attempt to avoid these reverses. All dualistic relations to 'the other', to 'the world' are attempts to quieten and deny the broken middle, the third term which arises out of misrecognition of desire, of work, of my and of your self-relation mediated by the self-relation of the other.

Secondly, this dialectic of misrecognition between two self-consciousnesses yields the meaning of *the law* that is inseparable from the meaning of *Bildung* (education, formation, cultivation), inseparable from the processes by which self-consciousness comes to learn its investment in denying the actuality of itself and other as always already engaged in some structure of recognition or misrecognition, in some triune (triple) relation to its own otherness and to the self-relating of the other. This is the meaning of *spirit* in Hegel, that short-hand term for the threefold state of the misrecognising parties. The law, therefore, is not *the superior term* which suppresses the local and contingent, nor is it *the symbolic* which catches every child in the closed circuit of its patriarchal embrace. The law is the falling towards or away from mutual recognition, the triune relationship, the middle, formed or deformed by reciprocal self-relations.

The law, therefore, in its actuality means full mutual recognition, 'spirit' or ethical life, but it can only be approached phenomenologically as it appears to us, modern legal persons, by expounding its dualistic reductions, when it is posited as modern legal status – the law of subjective rights separated from the law of the modern state. There is no word in the *Phenomenology* which appears in section titles as much as *the law* in all its various historical adventures – *the comedy of misrecognition*.

Thirdly and finally, to conclude by taking the subtitle of the

Conference on *Modernism* for which this chapter was first prepared: 'Politics, poetics, practice', I would say that it is this *poetics
of law*, where the worlds of recognition are tragic (*The Antigone*)
or comic (the modern hypertrophy of the subjective life), which
would permit us *to rediscover politics*: to work through the
mourning required by the disasters of modernity, to acknowledge
them as body by returning the spirit of misrecognition to its trinity
of full mutual recognition, instead of lamenting those disasters as
the universal 'spirit' of metaphysics, of the logocentric West. For if
'spirit' is understood dualistically, then 'nation', 'race', 'ethnicity'
can only be equally beholden to the contaminations (*sic*) of that
same metaphysics of subjectity, as Derrida argues. It cannot see
them as the ruse of pseudo-practices which, once again, demonise
self-relating otherness as 'the world'. Given the anxiety produced
by the self-opposition of subject to its substance, by the modern
evasion of mutual recognition attendant on the separation of subjective rights from the law of the modern state, intensified by the
individualism of post-modernity, to rediscover politics we need to
reconfigure the broken middle, not to deconstruct static dualisms.
As a propaedeutic to politics, I offer *the comedy of absolute spirit*
as *inaugurated* mourning: the recognition of our failures of full
mutual recognition, of the law which has induced our proud and
deadly dualisms, of the triune law – implicit but actual – which is
always at stake.

This comic approach – I cannot resist the provocation – would
also offer a deeper and more drastic alternative to the current
sacralising, commercialising and elevating into *raison d'état* as
well as Providential anti-reason of the Holocaust in America and
Israel.

4

'Would that they would forsake Me but observe my Torah': Midrash and political authority

PREFACE

While this chapter focuses on issues of Midrashism and Judaism as politics rather than ethics, it offers fundamental bearings on the conceptualisation of law. It proposes a model of doing politics as politics: 'the risk of action arising out of the negotiation of law', a revision of Hannah Arendt's discursive and antinomian idea of constitution-making. With the help of Pocock's civic republicanism, I launch a study of the Judaic body politic, a topic massively neglected in mainstream scholarship which has been promoting the Hebraic paradigm. This study draws on the *political* experience and wisdom of the Jews as embodied in their civic consciousness. It is *constitutional* rather than religious literacy that is here explored.

INTRODUCTION

The argument of this chapter falls into three parts. In the first part, I argue that Hartman's introduction of the idea of Midrash into literary culture does not constitute a form of prevalent anti-Hellenic Hebraism, but is a call for what he names 'religious literacy', which would introduce *discriminations* necessary to address the crisis of authority across the range from method in literary criticism to ethical and political theory. This distinguishes Hartman's *Judaica* from post-metaphysical *emblematisings* of Judaism as method and as ethics – all of which concur in presenting Judaism as undertaking *politics by other means*. In the second part of the chapter, I argue that Midrash in Judaism is not politics by other means but *politics per se*. Drawing on Pocock's *Machiavellian Moment* to reunify the source of the double dilemma of republican political authority – coercion and participation, or, *virtu* and virtue – I show that rabbinic Judaism's self-understanding as the politics of the three Crowns (*Ketarim*) displays a doubling of the double dilemma. For the double of Judaic polity has always been inserted within the double of the imperial or 'host' polity. Midrash, the exegesis of the three Crowns, becomes the way in which this insertion is negotiated and figured. Biblical, Mishnaic and Talmudic Midrash may be compared in this way; and their plasticity may be contrasted with modern, post-Napoleonic Judaic responses to the radically changed configuration of political authority. I begin to explore this contrast in the third part of the chapter. I conclude that any revival of Midrashic address to political authority demands what Hartman originally called in *The Unmediated Vision*, 'a method of complete interpretation', that is, 'a *unified multiplicity* of interpretation'. Only in this way is it possible to produce the *restitutive criticism*, which Hartman has more recently expounded, without also producing a reduction to the belligerents of *counter-identified multiplicity*, so-called 'cultural pluralism', for that is where the danger of aestheticising politics currently lies.

I

Let me begin with the most mighty gravamen that I have encountered in the critical literature. In a monumental study published recently entitled *The Rise of Eurocentrism: Anatomy of Interpretation*, Vassilis Lambropoulos argues that instead of responding to the aestheticising of politics by politicising *art* (according to Walter Benjamin's famous injunction), latter-day literary critics and philosophers have, on the one hand politicised *aesthetics*, producing 'the aesthetic theocracy of interpretation', while, on the other hand, they seek to protect both art and aesthetics from pan-appropriating politics.[1]

From Auerbach to Adorno and Horkheimer, to Derrida, Bloom[2] and Hartman, to Martin Bernal,[3] all these thinkers are said to operate according to what might be termed *neo-Hebraism*. This neo-Hebraism consists in the radical *uncoupling* of the age-old European hierarchy privileging Hebraism over Hellenism: the reverential coupling which has prevailed in traditional Christian culture and in modern Humanist and Protestant cultures, and which indicates the Hellenic investment in the Hebraic as its prophetic and ethical other. Neo-Hebraism has obtained a divorce from its formerly complementary other, the Hellenic, on the grounds that it is totalitarian, metaphysical reason. Responding to the collapse of the public covenant of interpretation, neo-Hebraism is said to afford 'the Yeshiva kind of sitting around', the contract of 'the consensus of commentary', attributed to Hartman; art as the remnant of prophetic redemption, attributed to Adorno; deconstruction as heterodox midrashic exegesis of exilic Writing and Law, attributed to Derrida, who is said also to collapse Oral Law into Written Law and Halacha into Scripture.[4]

The argument that neo-Hebraism has become the icon of the renewed politicisation of aesthetics (not of art) results in what would otherwise be nonsensical propositions regarding Hebraism, such as, 'the Hebraic triumph of the aesthetic',[5] for the ancient

Hebrews and rabbinic Judaism had no art or aesthetics – no representation of God. However, 'the aesthetic' refers here to the idealising of the interpretive or discursive community, of atoning criticism, of exilic Writing; in each case, a method which rests its claim to authority by evading the difficulty of authority as such – the legitimation of domination and its coercive means.

To my mind, Lambropoulos's enterprise is self-defeating in its architectonic and in its applications. Architectonically, drawing on Foucault, the author fails to locate his own authorship within the opposition of Hellenism and Hebraism which he has globalised. Most notably, the meaning of Hellenism and the ratiocination of his own argument, which seems consistently to deplore the Hebraicisation of literary and philosophical culture, are nowhere developed. As a result, although the three essays of which it consists are said to be non-cumulative, the book ends with a lame apostrophe to 'Some other kind of public virtue and political ethic' – for which, in spite of its apparent pro-Hellenism, it has disqualified the means of conception.

Lambropoulos's enterprise depends on the deconstruction of the contraries of Hellenism and Hebraicism and of art and politics, which have been extended so that they assimilate all the methods under examination. Instead of suffering within his own authorship the crisis of authority, the crisis of his own Hellenism, he documents everywhere else an oppositional investment which he has imposed. Nowhere is this more evident than in his misapprehension of Adorno and Horkheimer's *Dialectic of Enlightenment*. The guiding speculative proposition which the book unravels, 'Myth is already enlightenment; and enlightenment reverts to mythology', is taken by Lambropoulos as fatalistic and rhetorical evidence for 'the vile character' of reason and myth,[6] when it is a finely balanced proposition of the work of reason in myth and the incipient myth in unlimited reason – and of the necessity of placing one's own authorship in both of these positions. The lack of any account of transformed reason and politics, of any exposition of Hellenism, can be traced to this weakness throughout the central chapter of the book. With extensive historical and contemporary documentation, Lambropoulos has finally ruined the opposition of Athens and Jerusalem, Hellenism and Hebraism. While he can take no path himself, let us say that he opens up the path to the third city – the city which does not bear an emblematic name.

Geoffrey Hartman, it seems to me, has staked his authorship repeatedly against the politicising of aesthetics, while acknowledging that he writes from within the crisis in authority which makes that embellishing of the predicament concerning authority, that evasion of politics, so attractive. This is why his 'religious literacy'[7] cannot be taken as a neo-Hebraism; and why his reference to Midrash as method may be distinguished from presentations of Judaism as the sublime Other of modernity.

In his essay 'Art and Consensus in the Era of Progressive Politics', Hartman precisely sets himself against the confusion of criticism and political philosophy, the blandishments of aesthetic education, of a solely 'exegetical bonding', to which he judges that political philosophers from Kant and Schiller to Arendt and Rorty succumb when they expound 'the abstract and always unrealised vision of "a republic of letters" ', dissolving power by the model of conversation.[8] According to Hartman, criticism is the 'disintoxicant' which prevents the invocation of imaginative literature as self-transcendent empathy, as the vehicle of the extension of rights, as moment of multiculturalist conversion: 'the utopian premise . . . should not be allowed to cover up the difficult history we have passed through and are passing through'.[9]

It is in the light of this acknowledgment of our difficult history, of criticism's inability to solve the political problem, and of the discernment that political philosophers as much as literary critics have envisaged the cultural overcoming of politics, that Hartman's call for 'religious literacy' should be heard. His question 'How, then, can we bring the wealth of rabbinic wisdom [*hokhmah*], both halachah and aggadah, into the public domain?'[10] acknowledges both the crisis of the public domain (*traditum*) and the crisis in the transmission (*traditio*). It acknowledges the difficulty of translating the tradition into the public realm without making it into a technique or rhetoric of power, that is, without aestheticising politics, without abetting new Caesaropapism.[11]

To my mind, then, Beth Sharon Ash is wrong to attribute the conservative position to Hartman when she contrasts what she calls Hartman's and Bloom's 'modern theological criticism, rooted in both orthodox and heretical Judaism'.[12] Midrash cannot be understood as an unbroken line of Biblical commentary through which the tradition flows, but neither are the tradition and its transmission to be understood as intrinsic brokenness. Equally avoiding presenting Midrash as conservative, normative, unproblematic continuity or as radically antinomian, Kabbalistic discontinuity Hartman sees us as still failing towards what Kafka already expressed: 'the searching subtlety of midrash merges with images of modern self-doubt, whence a terrible ambivalence, both as attraction to and a repulsion from the all-pervasive mechanism of an unalterable law. Although that law builds fences around itself, Kafka's characters breach its perimeter: they cannot stay away despite the danger of proximity.'[13]

Hartman does not present Midrash as an alternative to politics; he presents it as the difficult integrity of ambivalence towards law and politics, a difficulty which may be comprehended, and a politics which remains with the danger of both the perimeter and the proximity, of acknowledging the boundary of the city and risking the anguish of the soul in breaching it and in being breached by it – the danger of renegotiating the boundaries of both the soul and the city and so altering the law of both, altering the un*alter*able by assuming the burden of being its *alter*, its other. This was the burden that the man from the country (*am ha'aretz* – the one who does not know the law) would not assume in the Midrash 'Before the Law' which the priest in the Cathedral relates towards the end of Kafka's *The Trial*. After decades of wasting away in front of the door to the law – the seemingly unalterable law with its unassailable keeper – the doorkeeper announces to the dying man 'this door is only for you. I am now going to shut it'. This is not to present Judaism as the alternative to monolithic domination but to outline why authority in crisis – the crisis which carries over from modernity to Judaism and from Judaism to modernity – requires political risk *greater* than that required in traditional society or traditional Judaism when the source of domination was not dispersed.

The persistent placing of his authorship within this difficult history is, I would claim, what distinguishes Hartman's *Judaica* from four other presentations of Judaism, each of which removes Judaism, as substance or as method, from politics, and thereby perpetuates the tradition of representing the meaning of Judaism as the achieving of *politics by other means*: Judaism as ethics (Levinas); Judaism as writing (Derrida); Judaism as Kabbalah and gnosis (Bloom); and Judaism as the Book of the Dead (Jabes).

For Hartman, the challenge is the risk of interpretation, the negotiation of difficult history. He asks 'Do we have the strength to enter or to emerge from that *pardes*?'[14] *Pardes* is a mnemonic, the initials of four kinds of biblical interpretation: *Peshat* – literal; *Remez* –

MOURNING BECOMES THE LAW

allegorical or philosophical; *Derash* – aggadic; and *Sod* – mystical. *Pardes* is also the name of a strange garden. In the Tractate of the Babylonian Talmud, *Hagigah*, which deals with the celebration of holidays in Temple worship, there is a very short story:

> Four entered the garden [*Pardes*] namely Ben Azzai, Ben Zoma, Aher and Rabbi Akiva. Rabbi Akiva said to them: When you arrive at the (place of the) stones of pure marble, don't say, Water, Water! Because it is said: He who speaks falsehood will not stand before My eyes (Psalms 101:7). Ben Azzai looked and died. Scripture says about him: Blessed in the eyes of the Lord is the death of His righteous (Psalms 116:15). Ben Zoma looked and was afflicted. Scripture says about him: If you have found honey, eat (only) your fill, because if you become surfeited, you will vomit (Proverbs 25:16). Aher cut the shoots. Rabbi Akiva departed in peace.[15]

This tale has had many interpretations. Rabbi Akiba (or Akiva) was the greatest rabbi of the Mishnaic period who arranged and preserved the Oral Law and developed a novel mode for its inter-pretation. It was by virtue of his activity, prior to the Bar Kochba revolt of 135 CE that the Mishnah could later be compiled. In addition, Rabbi Akiba was a consummate politician, negotiating with, and respected by the Romans; he became the only rabbi of stature to oppose the Roman decree prohibiting the study of the law and to support Bar Kochba in the last great military attempt by the Jews to overthrow Roman rule. The three other rabbis named in the story were all disciples of Akiba: Ben Azzai, Ben Zoma and Aher. The story is generally held to indicate that Ben Azzai and Ben Zoma tended to mysticism and lost their minds in attempting to employ reason to penetrate the mysteries of God, prompted by their desire to understand the sufferings of the Jews – for which the Romans taunted the Sages. The rabbi known as

'Aher' – the one who is different – became alienated from Judaism as a result of his mystical divagations and aided the Romans in defeating the Jews and their scholars. Only Rabbi Akiba, it would seem, was able to combine self-limiting mysticism with innovative approaches to the Oral Law and with supple politics of negotiation, opposition and, ultimately, revolt. As a result of his support for Bar Kochba, he was imprisoned and eventually killed in an especially gruesome manner.[16]

This is not *politics by other means: this is politics* – the risk of action arising out of the negotiation of the law. Rabbi Akiba departed in peace – while the two gnostics and the one who went into exile succumbed.

II

It was Franz Rosenzweig who argued in the third part of *The Star of Redemption* that Judaism left its holy war behind in its antiquity and became a sanctified community outside the course of world history, which remains the arena of Christian mission. In spite of its apparent privileging of Judaism, Rosenzweig's eschatological history of the world, according to which Judaism and Christianity together configure the pre-history of redemption,[17] reproduces another version of Christian supercessionism, while it denies the tradition of universal world mission to the 'chosen' people. From Benjamin's Messianism to Levinas's ethics of Otherwise than Being, *The Star of Redemption* has provided a new source and authority for the separation of divine, bloodless violence from the bloody, partial violences of the law of the world, the separation of ethics from coercion. In the central part of *The Star of Redemption*, the divine commandment to love is expounded as the only commandment, if instantly obeyed, that cannot become law, that cannot coerce.

This desire to conceive of coercion and law as absolutely distinct from the good and the community (already encountered as the uncoupling of Hellenism and Hebraism) represents one of the main ways in which modern Jewish thought participates in a methodological and substantive divorce which characterises the development of modern philosophy in its separation of ethics from the social analysis of the ways in which authority is legitimised. This epochal difficulty in relating the analysis of the operations of modern power – its techniques and its technologies – to the reflection on the nature and actuality of the good, which has given rise to the intellectual division of labour between philosophy and political sociology, has especial consequences for the comprehension of Jewish history and the meaning of Judaism. For, as I shall outline below, the rabbinic conceptualisation of the organization of ordained and therefore legitimate authorities has to be seen as the negotiation and promotion of the good and the legitimation of coercive institutions, that is, as the politics of the Judaic body politic, or *Edah*, in an autonomous, divinely mandated representation when it is, in effect, constituted within the heteronomous context of the environing suzerainty. The representation or plundering of Judaism as ethical is a double retreat from this double dilemma of Jewish history up to the modern period.

What we have come to accept as a *categorical methodological precept* or rule – with its justification in the distinction of fact from value and of social analysis from political commendation – *viz.*, the separation of types of legitimate authority from judgements concerning the goals or values of the exercise of power, knowledge of coercion from practical interest in the good, has itself a history. This history comprises the difficulty, intrinsic to the political tradition from the ancient polis to the modern republican state, of relating political goals to means, the idea of the good to the reality of the monopoly of the means of legitimate violence. Sections of Weber's *Economy and Society*, for example, the section on 'Political Communities' at the end of the *Sociology of Law*, can easily be read as if they were addressed to Machiavelli's Prince: they concern the ways in which power, defined as the successful monopoly of the means of legitimate violence within a given territory, may be obtained, maintained, routinised and, *a fortiori*, lost; they may be read, that is, as a cynical handbook for the manipulation of power, regardless of any concern for the good.

The difference between Machiavelli and Weber is that when we read *Economy and Society*,[18] we consider we are engaging in value-free social science, but when we read *The Prince*, we consider we are receiving a canny, unethical set of instructions for the exercise of power. Both ways of reading are wrong, for what Pocock says about Machiavelli applies equally to Weber: their realism about power must be taken in the light of their commitment to values – the idea of the republic or the atrophy of substantive politics, respectively. I would like to suggest that Pocock's *Machiavellian Moment*[19] could equally well imply *the Weberian Moment*: that Weber, like Machiavelli, understands the dilemma of legal-rational politics to consist in the imposition of form (on Fortuna) *and* as inner brokerage or the participation of virtuous citizens in the good. Weber's distinction between formal and substantive rationality may then be seen as a methodological transliteration of the historical difficulty of aspiring to and representing the good between citizens when the political community is bounded in both time and space – by its own origin in time and by its juxtaposition in space to other polities, 'the world of unlegitimated power relations' (as Pocock expresses, it using Weberian conceptuality)[20] – both of which may give rise to corrupt, delegitimated internal and external relations. For Weber, the increasing prevalence of instrumental rationality over substantive rationality has its history in the development of capitalism and the Protestant ethic. The splitting of the rationalisation of everyday life from the erstwhile interest in salvation does not bestow total control on the Weberian Prince, but produces inner anxiety and political paralysis.

Pocock suggests himself that *the Machiavellian Moment* could be extended to Rousseau, *the Rousseauian Moment*, as it were, 'in the sense that he [Rousseau] dramatically and scandalously pointed out a contradiction [in the idea of the republic] that others were trying to live with' (p. 504). Indeed, the inconsistencies between the *Second* and *Third Discourses* and the incompatibilities between the normative and historical sections of the *Social Contract* could be comprehended in terms of legitimate, unlegitimate and unlegitimisable boundaries, in terms, that is, of *virtù* and virtue. I propose that, if Rousseau is the Machiavelli of the eighteenth century, then Weber is the Machiavelli of the early twentieth century: an ultimate concern with the political good – with goal or value rationality – is overshadowed by the analysis of the realities of formal or instrumental rationality, the legal-rational type of authority and its legitimate employment of the means of violence.

Ethics and domination, the good and violence, the community and the law, do not belong to two worlds, to two cities, to two different methodologies. The counter-distinction of ethics from politics is itself the effect, the result, the outcome, the mediation, of the relation between the negotiated meaning of the Good, whether ancient virtue or modern freedom, and the historical actualities of institutional configurations.

In the light of this excursus, it could be argued that the major difficulty of Judaic political self-representation – that it has had to accommodate a heteronomous political environment, while still understanding itself as an autonomous legal and political system, expressed by the rabbinic dictum, *dina malkuta dina* (the law of the land is law) – represents not a doubling of the double *Machiavellian Moment*, according to which the Judaic tension between the substance and form of the good is multiplied by the parallel tension within the host or hostile polity, but, on the contrary, that Judaism has lived in fuller awareness than other polities of the ways in which the violence of non-legitimisable temporal and spatial boundaries rebounds into the collective and would-be sovereign definition of and commitment to the good (here, the kingdom-to-come). This might be considered the overcoming of the *Machiavellian Moment* by the institutional recognition of it.

While recent philosophical presentations of Judaism have become increasingly ethical, gnostic, memorial or mystical, the most recent scholarship of biblical and formative Judaism applies Weberian analysis of domination to the midrashic legitimations of changing political configurations. I am thinking here of Michael Fishbane, Jacob Neusner and Daniel Elazar and Stuart Cohen, on whose work I will be drawing in what follows.

Since God is the king of every Judaism, it might be imagined that there can be no political representation and that there is no need for legitimation of authority – for theocracy is intrinsically self-legitimated and self-legitimising. However, rabbinic political theory in the Mishnah, the origins of which are in Scripture, presents the constitution of the three Crowns (*Ketarim*) which has prevailed from the end of the Second Commonwealth to today. The origin and persistence of this framework itself derives from rabbinic accession to political authority and on rabbinic use and development of Midrash.

I am using 'Midrash' in its most extensive definition, syn-
onymous with 'exegesis', since this encompasses the widest range
of Judaic institutions and raises the widest range of issues. Four
meanings of 'Midrash' need to be distinguished:

1 Exegesis in the sense of intra-biblical exegesis, *halachic* and
   aggadic, and of halachic and aggadic exegesis in the texts of
   formative Judaism (Mishnah, Tosefta, Jerusalem Talmud). In
   this sense there is *halachic* and *aggadic* Midrash.

2 (More restrictively), exegesis of Scripture – either the line by
   line relating of Mishnah to Scripture (the Babylonian
   Talmud), or the line by line exegesis of Scripture or the discursive exegesis of Scripture. In this sense there is no
   Midrash in the Mishnah.

3 The main collection of Scriptural exegesis over 1,500 years,
   closed *c.* 600 CE, known as *Midrash Rabbah* – Great
   Midrash – on Genesis, Exodus, Leviticus, Numbers,
   Deuteronomy, Lamentations, Ruth, Ecclesiastes, Esther,
   Song of Songs.

4 Medieval collections of Midrashim (about which I know
   nothing).[21] In order to avoid Hellenising, Latinising or mod-
   ernising Judaic political institutions, I propose to follow
   Cohen and Elazar and introduce Hebrew terms.

In sketching the constitution of the three Crowns (*Ketarim*), I
would like to demonstrate that Judaism, in its legitimation of the
unequal institutional *sharing* of the means of political violence[22]
(Weber's definition of the maintenance of the authority of the state
or political community is its successful *monopoly* of the means of
legitimate violence) has been channelled and expressed by

Midrashim, and that it is this mode of expression of its difficult history that has conferred the ethical aura on Judaism's literatures and practices. This 'sharing' of legitimate authority and hence of the means of violence has two sets of meanings: one, the separation and sharing of powers (*Ketarim*) represented as autonomous or sovereign Judaic self-government; two, the plasticity of that same framework of the three Crowns (*Ketarim*) in incorporating, by subordinate representation, the heteronomous or suzerain government, so that the range of respective distribution of power from the Second Commonwealth maximum, *imperium in imperio*, to the minimum, for example, the imposed charters and *servi camerae regis* (servants of the royal household) of the period of the Crusades, could be encompassed within its triangle.[23]

Rabbinic political theory of the Mishnah – the period of destruction of political independence after Bar Kochba, 135 CE – articulates theocracy or government by God, shared and made mutual by the political covenant (*Berit*) between God and humanity, and further diffused by the franchise of kings, prophets and priests.[24] The notional existence of three Crowns (*Ketarim*), 'each endowed with its own divine mandate to participate in national rulership' (p. 3), expresses the distribution of political authority. The three ordained authorities or Crowns are the *Keter Torah*, the *Keter Kehunah* (priesthood) and the *Keter Malkhut* (kingship):

> As thus ordained, the domain of the *torah* constitutes the vehicle whereby God's teachings to Israel are interpreted, specified and transmitted; the *kehunah*, the conduit whereby God and his people are brought into constant contact and close proximity; the *malkhut*, the legitimately empowered means whereby civic relationships are structured and regulated in accordance with the requirements of Mosaic law. (p. 14)

In Biblical times the Hebrews had been ruled by a prophet (Moses), by a king (David) and by a priest (Ezra). This constitutional theory, with its apparent equilibrium of institutional power sharing between prophet, priest and king, was developed, however, when Judaism was politically devastated, and never again to have a king or temple priesthood, nor to be politically autonomous. It was articulated, that is, by the non-legitimate authority of the Tannaitic Rabbis, who legitimised their effective monopoly of the means of violence by rearranging the triad of the *Ketarim* so that the jurisdiction of the *Keter Torah*, scholarship, was situated at the apex of the triangle. The Rabbis arrogated, that is, prophetic authority to themselves; 'the result was to "rabbinise" the prophets', developing a mode of exegesis which is strikingly silent on the virtual power and organization of their own invisible college.[25]

However, the constitutional blueprint of the three triangulated *Ketarim* has provided Judaism with a plasticity of self-representation over the epochs of its difficult history that has made it possible to articulate the actualities of the legitimate and non-legitimate employment of the means of violence – sovereign and suzerain.

This fundamental triangle remains unchanged; the effect of changing suzerainty on the organization of legitimate authority (unequal sharing of the means of violence) can be represented on the internal as well as the external boundaries of the triangle below.[26]

Elazar and Cohen number the epochs of the Jewish Polity up to the establishment of the state of Israel. Although the modern state of Israel is not a theocracy, the diagram can accommodate that, and the authors pay equal attention to post-war Diaspora Jewry, from America to Argentina, France and Iran.[27] It could be argued, therefore, that they are working with the classic rabbinic notion

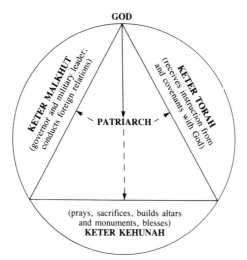

Figure 3

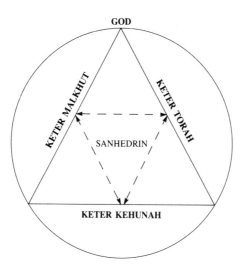

Figure 4 Constitutional representation

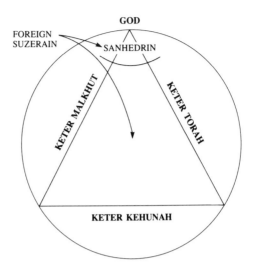

Figure 5 After failure of Great Rebellion of 70 CE. Here
Sanhedrin power has shrivelled and a foreign suzerain
effectively rules.

according to which each Jewry understands itself as 'Israel', that
is, as a sanctified community, holy and apart, living a sanctified life
for the sake of the kingdom to come,[28] rather than *as a modern
religion*, practised according to private inclination and interest by
individuals defined as legal persons, bearers of rights and duties
(not as members of pre-modern corporations), within the boundaries of civil society separated from the modern state. When
Napoleon summoned a Sanhedrin to Paris, French Jewry partici-
pated in his transformation of Judaism into 'a religion', with a cler-
ical hierarchy modelled on the Church.[29]

For Judaism, the fundamental political differences effected by the
modern separation of state and civil society are that the restrictions
on movement and on the control of property, according to which
Judaism has always had to counter-define itself, are removed – each
individual now has in principle and in law control over his or her

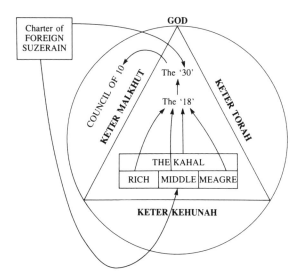

Figure 6 Kehillah of Barcelona, fourteenth century. An
example of shared power between Sanhedrin and foreign
suzerain, represented by a Charter.

movement and his or her property and his or her belief. To my mind,
this casts into question the validity of the triangular mode of representation because, paradoxically, the non-legitimate gaps no longer
exist – the gaps where the rabbis omitted themselves in a representation of legitimate authority (sharing of the means of violence) which
presupposed no freedom of movement, limited control over property, but full control over the transfer of women. The most intransi-
gent disputes between Napoleon and the delegates of French Jewry
concerned interfaith marriage and this remained the one issue on
which French Jews refused to yield to Napoleon's demand.

III

Why, then, do we wish to modernise Midrash as *method*? And
what is at stake in the idea of enriching the public domain with rab-

binic *wisdom*? Should the idea of Midrash as method be understood as the idealising of the plasticity of Judaic *traditio* in relation
to its *traditum*, of its transmission in relation to its established
authority?[30] Does the turn to multiple midrashic interpretation
indicate a turn away from the purportedly monolithic domination
of non-negotiable reason? Does the ambition to enrich the public
domain with rabbinic wisdom (*Hokhmah*) posit the political community exclusively in terms of ethical discursivity or conversation?

These aims are not correctly imputed to Hartman's mobilisation
of Midrash, for the very imputation implies a fundamental failure
to comprehend both Judaism and modernity: it rests on a
characterisation of the politics of modernity to which he does not
subscribe, while it is unable to identify Judaism as a political tradition. To oppose Midrash to the monolithic domination of reason
would be to simplify the difficult history of Judaism and of modernity; it would amount to using Midrash to deny one's own interest
in power by idealising method and ethics beyond domination.

On the argument developed here, the attention to Midrash and
to rabbinic wisdom should make it possible to uncover that difficult history, whether the period of formative Judaism, late antiquity, or the modern period. Judaism developed as a more or less
negotiated relationship between inner and outer domination;
Midrash as the means by which multiple external and internal
domination was legitimised as authority. Whatever the conditions
of suzerainty, Midrash perpetuated Judaism as 'Israel', as a coercive legal actuality within the messianic belief in the kingdom to
come – the advent of the kingdom implying universal justice
without non-legitimate boundaries between hostile polities.
Political virtue was preserved as the tradition under conditions
where political *virtù*, domination, was manifold and manifest on
the inner and outer boundaries of the polity.

There has been no Judaic ethics without there simultaneously being a non-Judaic politics. The continuing debate between *halachic* (orthodox) and conservative (reform) Judaism over whether *halacha* needs ethical supplementation presupposes the politics of modernity which neither party to the debate is able to concede or qualified to address. For Judaism *as a religion* in civil society is no longer engaged in the unequal sharing (even less the monopoly) of the means of legitimate violence – it is no longer *a community* in the sense that it no longer possesses any means of coercion. The separation of the modern state from civil society disperses authority – it does not concentrate it: this is reflected within Judaism by the fundamental contestation of the *traditio*, the mode of transmission, as well as the *traditum*, the established authority, which has led to the development of several modern Judaisms – *halachic*, reform, *hassidic*, and so on. (Could this be comparable to the diverse Judaisms of the Hellenistic and Roman period – Pharisee, Essene, Philo, Christian – prior to the unifying development of normative, rabbinic Judaism in the wake of the Christianising of the Empire?)

Under these modern circumstances, Midrash can tell the truth about its loss of truth, its loss of the law, and about the attempt of the individual to transact the relations of civil society: is she less equipped to live outside the law or more equipped – since loss and multiple authority have always been the presuppositions of Judaism? Modern politics offers no unified focus of domination: the boundaries which separate the state from civil society and *Innerlichkeit* from the rational, methodical organisation of everyday life are now drawn within each individual, while the non-legitimated boundaries between states still corrupt the inner boundaries, now located within each individual soul producing the modern phantasies of exclusive monopolising of the means of violence, which take the shape of racism, fascism, religious and ethnic exclusivity.

This is why *restitutive criticism*[31] demands 'a method of complete interpretation' – a unified multiplicity of interpretation[32] – for its contrary, criticism of counter-identifying restitution, of cultural multiplicity or cultural pluralism, will, in its turn, absolutise a minor literature, a tradition, a people, and remove them from the dynamic of actuality. Even though the abstract, formal, legal equality of modernity produces systematic inequality for specific social and cultural classes of people, to promote that classification as restitution is to fix it. For the boundary stake of abstract legality not only pierces the individual soul but renders invisible the actuality of others, their work, desire and otherness, as well as oneself as other, and it is this anguish which makes phantasy projections of community, secured by an idealised outer boundary of religion, nation, so compelling. To arrest one's self-understanding in a classification is to prevent the development of mutual recognition – it is to aestheticise politics.

In his essay 'Criticism and Restitution', Hartman argues that Hegelian recognition, the struggle for recognition between lord and bondsman, is the only way restitutive criticism can avoid the counter-identification of literatures, which would 'reinstate once again the contested notion of privilege as well as essentialist – and at worst, racialist – slogans that have bedeviled an era of catastrophic nationalism'.[33] One might call this appeal to Hegel *the Hegelian Moment*: the struggle for recognition is a drama in which the good (full mutual recognition) and the means (the varieties of misrecognition) engender each other and may be negotiated but only by acknowledgement of mutual implication in the violence of misrecognition.

Paradoxically, the loss of truth, the loss of focused authority or even of plastic authority, and the concomitant internalisation of authority, requires what Hegel called *absolute method* (intending the terms to cancel themselves out), and what Hartman calls *complete interpretation*. The unified multiplicity of interpretation implies the dynamic of difficult history, while the counter-identified multiplicity imposes a static determination on that history. The complete interpretation, which, in bare outline, I have attempted to practise here, reconstructs *how the limitation has come about*, and, in so doing, it aims to undermine the idea that domination is categorical, and resistance only viable as reassertion of identity fixed under the terms of the original exclusion.

Martin Buber and Elie Wiesel and, I hope, countless others, relate a Hassidic tale about the progressive loss of a prayer and its transmission: by telling the tale of this loss they produce a Midrash on the Midrash, a new transmission contrary to the tradition of loss:

> When the great Israel Baal Shem Tov saw misfortune threatening the Jews, it was his custom to go into a certain part of the forest to meditate. There he would light a fire, say a special prayer, and the miracle would be accomplished and the misfortune averted.
>
> Later, when his disciple, the celebrated Maggid of Mezeritch, had occasion, for the same reason, to intercede with heaven, he would go to the same place in the forest and say: 'Master of the Universe, listen! I do not know how to light the fire, but I am still able to say the prayer.' And again the miracle would be accomplished.
>
> Still later, Moshe-Leib of Sassov, in order to save his people once more, would go into the forest and say : 'I do not know the prayer, but I know the place and this must be sufficient.' It was sufficient and the miracle was accomplished.
>
> Then it fell to Israel of Rizhin to overcome misfortune. Sitting in his armchair, his head in his hands, he spoke to God: 'I am unable to light the fire and I do not know the prayer; I cannot even find the place in the forest. All I can do is tell the story, and this must be sufficient.' And it was sufficient.

It no longer is. The proof is that the threat has not been averted. Perhaps we are no longer able to tell the story. Could all of us be guilty? Even the survivors? Especially the survivors?[34]

The tale plus the comment which questions the continuing ability to tell the tale is the tale renewed by the questioning of its transmission in spite of the loss of its truth. Not to tell the tale of *perhaps* not being able to tell the tale would make the loss of the tale and the occurrence of the catastrophe absolute: it would fix the catastrophe as the meaning, or, rather, as the devastation, of meaning. Here the commentary only ventures: 'Perhaps we are no longer able to tell the story', having told the tale and, in its spirit, having added another, albeit radical, diminution to its series. 'Could all of us be guilty . . . Especially the survivors?' This could be heard as: 'we cannot tell the tale because we are guilty'. Could this be the age-old prophetic trope: the catastrophe was not averted because we turned away from God? (Even that response of self-blame has the psychic and political function of asserting one's own agency in the face of disaster.) Or are we guilty for surviving when six million died? God forbid! We would be guilty if we remain self-defined *solely* as survivors; 'guilty' because fixed in a counter-identification. To survive – to live again – demands a new tale : a new prayer to be found, a new polity to be founded. It demands a willingness to participate in power and its legitimate violence for the sake of the good. Not as a sanctified, holy Israel, nor as Israeli, or any other, *raison d'état*, but as the risk of recognition – the risk of coming to discover the self-relation of the other as the challenge of one's own self-relation.

I have told the tale. Midrash is not beautiful, it is difficult.

5

Potter's Field: death worked
and unworked

When morning was come, all the chief priests and elders of the
people took counsel against Jesus to put him to death:
And when they had bound him, they led *him* away, and
delivered him to Pontius Pilate the governor.
Then Judas, which had betrayed him, when he saw that he was
condemned, repented himself, and brought again the thirty
pieces of silver to the chief priests and elders,
Saying, I have sinned in that I have betrayed the innocent blood.
And they said, What *is that* to us? see thou *to that*.
And he cast down the pieces of silver in the temple, and went
and hanged himself.
And the chief priests took the silver pieces, and said, It is not lawful
for to put them into the treasury, because it is the price of blood.
And they took counsel, and bought with them the potter's field,
to bury strangers in.
Wherefore that field was called, The field of blood, unto this day.
Then was fulfilled that which was spoken by Jeremiah the
prophet, saying,
And they took the thirty pieces of silver, the price of him that
was valued, whom they of the children of Israel did value;
And gave them for the potter's field, as the Lord appointed me.

Matthew 27: 1–10

I

Today, in the middle of the Atlantic Ocean, lies an island called *Potter's Field*. There, on fresh winds, the foul blood of New York City is transported. For that acre of blood affords the only *columbarium* for the ashes of the unclaimed, derelict dead of the city – for unidentified murdered bodies, for paupers, and now, for the new category of destitution: those who die of AIDS in the *triage* wards of the city hospitals.

New York City, 16 May 1992: the body of my love has been taken to Potter's Field, taken outside the walls of the city; beyond the ramparts, his ungodly ashes will have been scattered upon that collective grave for the unreprieved – without community, without commemoration and hence without end.

Yet, by decreeing this merciless disposal, the city reclaims his soul – and mine. Without proper burial and mourning, he cannot rest, and I cannot recommence. He belonged body and soul, in his manner of living and in his manner of dying, to the *polis*. According to Plato, the tripartite soul, which consists of reason, appetite and *Thumos*, the principle of high spirits, ally or enemy of reason and desire, corresponds to the inner constitution and inner warfare of the city. We always knew we owed the purity *and* the contamination of our love to the splendour and the misery of that city – to its laws and to its anarchies.

Since mourning refuses to become me, should I then follow the wife of Phocion[1] and, with a trusted woman companion to keep guard, steal away from the city to that abominable and abominated island, abyss of the city itself, there to gather the cursed ashes of my love, to give them a tomb, a resting place in my own body, to release his soul, and mine, too, from the agon of interminable wandering? To inaugurate by consuming his ashes the long-overdue work of mourning, in a pitiable reversal of that work which, in the normal course of events, takes place within the city. Then to incorporate the dead one into one's own body and soul is to refuse the work of mourning, to refuse, in melancholy, to let go.

If all meaning is mourning, and mourning (or absence) must become our norm (or presence) for there to be morning (dawning or future), and *not* interminable dying, then all meaning and all mourning belong to the city, to the *polis*.

In Poussin's painting, *Gathering the Ashes of Phocion*, Phocion's wife bends down outside the boundary wall of Athens to scoop up his ashes, in an integral *gestus* which gathers her own soul and body into this act of perfect devotion. The tension of political defiance and the fear of being discovered appear only in the taut *contrapposto* of the woman servant, which is juxtaposed to the utter vulnerability of the stooping wife. Arising above the two foregrounded figures is a combined land- and townscape of classical magnificence with gleaming temples and municipal buildings, perfect displays of the architectural orders, which convey no hint of malign intent. Yet Phocion's condemnation and manner of dying were the result of tyranny temporarily usurping good rule in the city. Does Poussin's representation, taken from Plutarch's *Life of Phocion*, oppose pure, individual love to impure, worldly injustice?[2]

To participate body and soul in our relationships and in our self-identity in the work and in the undoing of the city and yet to be deprived of, or to refuse, the work of mourning has *political consequences*. It tempts us to oppose pure, gratuitous love to the injustice of the world; to see ourselves as suffering but good, and the city as evil. As a result, we are no longer able to chant with Antigone: 'Because we suffer we acknowledge we have erred.' This opposing of our cherished good to public ill denies the third term which gives meaning to both judgements – the just city and the just act, the just woman and the just man. In Poussin's painting *this transcendent but mournable justice* is configured, its absence given presence, in the architectural perspective which frames and focuses the enacted justice of Phocion's wife, her response to the implied act of injustice by the city. To see the built forms themselves as ciphers of the unjust city would be to perpetuate endless dying and endless tyranny – unending disaster.

In Blanchot's *oeuvre* death and dying are interminable; he invents a new mode of mourning, which does not involve working through, nor acceptance of, the inevitable negation by which meaning is secured against an always absent world. Mourning in Blanchot becomes *poesis* or 'making', which is the elegy to Orpheus, hymn and witness to incessant *désoeuvrement* – Being without work. For Blanchot, the letting go of mourning is not for morning or dawning, for commencing, but for the endless reality of ending, which our workful beginnings can only, and must always, violate.

Blanchot's immense and multiform elegy to death as *désoeuvrement* not only takes place outside the city walls, it takes place beyond the cosmos: it is the writing of the disaster – *dés-astres*: the stars torn out – beyond the music of the intelligent, ordered heavenly spheres, and hence beyond any conceivable, intramundane political order. Even less does it concern the tripartite soul, analogue of the city, whose reason, appetite and high spirit (*Thumos*), engaged in work and in mourning, have no access to unbounded, incessant dying.

No work, no city, no soul – this *aberrant* mourning of endless ending is, nevertheless, *a work of the city and of the soul*. It is a mourning which, like mine, has been banished beyond the city walls; there it has substituted its pain, its agon, its barren and lyrical gestures, its reflections in poetry and prose, *its writing*, for *the justice which it has vowed to renounce.*

II

Lazare, veni foras (Lazarus, come forth)[3]
John 11: 43

This rebirth of Lazarus, this miracle of faith – Christ's and Lazarus's – this difficult return to difficult life, is presented by Blanchot as the quintessence of 'the murder', 'the immense hecatomb', which summons 'the dark cadaverous reality from its primordial depths and in exchange gave it only the life of the mind . . . and not the intimacy of the unrevealed'.[4] Language, according to Blanchot, brings into being by negation, but 'the torment of language is what it lacks because of the necessity that it be the lack of precisely this. It cannot even name it.' It can be no accident that Blanchot selects Lazarus's return *from* death as a return *to* death, in two senses: by being named, something is murdered; by coming forth, Lazarus returns to 'the impossibility of dying'. In these two senses, Blanchot focuses on what Lazarus loses and to what he is restored, but not on the difficulty to which he miraculously, *non-naturally*, accedes: the supernatural difficulty of natural life.

What is this *impossibility* of dying – in living, in language and in literature?

> The proverbial formula 'as soon as one is born one is old enough to die', is certainly impressive to the extent that it distributes randomly over the course of life the possibility of mortality. However, in this formula there is still an easy relationship between life and death: dying remains a possibility – a power which is attributed to life or which is verified in life and confirmed in death – determined thus between two terms (one begins to die with the beginning which is the start of life – the

expulsion of birth being metaphorically inverted into an
overturning encounter with a kind of death – and with which
one finishes by finishing with life, the cadaverous equality or, to
go further, to the ultimate great rest, the entropic equality of the
universe). But perhaps dying has no determinate relationship
with living, with the reality, the presence of 'life'. A pure
phantasm, perhaps, a joke of which no trace materializes in the
present, or even a folly which overturns being from top to
bottom and, at the same time, only reaches us as an
imperceptible neurosis, escaping all observation, invisible
because too visible. Thus writing perhaps: a writing which would
not be a possibility of speech (no more than dying is not a
possibility of life) – a murmur however, a folly however, which is
played on the silent surface of language.   (*Le pas au delà*)[5]

If to die (*mourir*) is not a *possibility*, facility or power, then to
propose that to die is *impossible* is to rejoin and reaffirm the metaphysical opposition of possibility and actuality which is putatively
under erasure. To propose that to die is *repetition* falls to the totalising, numerical, serial connotation of 'repetition' which Blanchot
discerns even in Nietzsche's eternal return (pp. 133, 151, 22, 33,
54). To hear the commandment that it is *forbidden* to die is to hear
'constantly in us, not as a call of obligation to live, but as the voice
itself breaking each time the commandment'. The horror of the
death camps and of the millions dying 'makes each dying guilty
even when never more innocent'. 'Possibility', 'repetition', 'commandment', 'event' – language is dissolved in the attempt to name
this one thing on which it depends, and which it therefore cannot
name or describe (pp. 13–14).

In italics: '*To die – dying in the cold and the dissolution of the
Outside: always outside oneself as outside life*'(p. 134). Can this
discourse of *externality* escape any more than any other the twin
paradoxes, one, of collapsing back into its metaphysical partner

(the Inside, warmth, immanence) so that, once again, dying becomes the logical and existential double of living; or, two, the destruction of actuality which must take place for the name to arise? In addition to the difficulty of naming and situating *dying*, the difficulty of thinking *dying* appertains to its temporality, its futurity, or the tense of its verb, since it cannot be simply past or perfected – that would be 'to be dead [*être-mort*]' (p. 151). All verb tenses are gathered in the impossibility of this thinking of return: 'that which has happened without traces and which it would be always necessary to wait for from the empty infinity of the future' (p. 151). This formula could equally well be taken as a parable of *the kingdom of God*, for the kingdom, too, has happened, is happening and is always yet to happen. Or, as John Henry Newman proposed, in an alleviation of verb tension that distinguishes the Saints from Christ: 'The Saints are ever failing from the earth and Christ is all but coming':

> Death delivers from death – Perhaps only from dying. – Dying is this lightness on this side of all freedom from which nothing is liberated. – What frightens without doubt in death, contrary to the analyses of antiquity: death does not have in itself anything to appease death; it is as if therefore it would survive itself, in the impossibility of being which it disperses, without this impotence taking the form of lack of completion – lack of accomplishment – proper or improper to dying. – The exteriority of being, when it takes the name of death, of dying, of the relation to the other, or perhaps of speech when that is not retracted in the manner of speaking, does not permit any relationship (not of identity, nor of alterity) with itself. – With exteriority, speech is given perhaps absolutely and for absolutely multiple, but in such a way that it [exteriority] could not develop in speech: always already lost, without usage and even such that what is lost in it (the essence of the lost that it measures) does not claim, by a reversal, that something – a gift, an absolute gift – is magnified or designated

in the loss itself. – *I do not have therefore the right to say anything. – Certainly, no right at all.* (*Le pas au delà*, p. 180)

The second half of this paragraph provides guidance for the first – unappeased, ever-surviving, impotent, dispersing, the being of death is captured by epithets which are normally employed as its contraries (death is appeasement, non-survival, capacity, concentration of an event of nothingness) in order to erase the logic of relationship with itself, of identity and alterity, which must be implied in any idea of self-relation by which something is identified. Yet sharing the marker of 'exteriority', speech (but not death or the relation to the other), is only given absolutely (that is, without relation or self-identity), not as something which will be developed in speech, but instead as an absolute loss in relation to which speech cannot be understood as the contrary – as the magnified gain. This prompts the abrupt, intrusive, first-person confession in italics that therefore 'I' do not have the right to say anything (for nothing can be claimed by right or developed in speech – it can only be hymned in writing), emphasised by the insistent '*Certainly, no right*'.

Two crimes are indicated by the strange incursion of litigious terms: murder and illegitimate right. The use of a dialectic of *terms* in a double negation – *not* the magnified contrary of loss and gift – cannot be justified as the expression of the in*term*inable, hence the exclamation 'I do not have therefore the right to say anything'. The idea of death can only be insinuated by referring to its contrary characteristics – unappeasement, survival, impotence – and in so doing advertising *the murder*. For we could not understand even inappropriate epithets and the substantive to which they point without the logic of self-alterity and identity, without, that is, committing the murder which bestowed on Lazarus 'only the life of the mind . . . not the intimacy of the unrevealed'. Dying and death, even in the guarded ratiocination and lyricism of this writing, have been usurped by spurious right in being spoken of, and murdered by being thematised. Moreover, these crimes are committed in an active and reflexive labour of form.

'Exteriority' is hymned under many names in *The Space of Literature*: 'the Gaze of Orpheus', 'the Original Experience', and several sets of non-contrary doubles: 'the other night', 'the other day', 'the other death', 'two versions of the imaginary'. All these *murders*, these illegitimate *rights*, presuppose *the disaster* – they evince the disturbed, gnostic (I use *gnostic* and not *mystical* advisedly), the *gnostic* relation to law and to the idea of law which comes with perennial expulsion from the city, and now with contemporaneous destruction in the death-camps, from surviving and not surviving outside the city; at the same time, the inconsistent introduction of litigious terms, such as 'murder' and 'right', shows that the memory of the law of the city has not faded so completely that its juridical actions cannot be invoked.

III

Orpheus is not Dionysus.[6] Orphism was 'a reformulation and reformation of Dionysiac religion', even while it returned to a type of religion more primitive than prevailing Olympianism. Orphism and Dionysian religion involve two different types of immortality and of individuation. Dionysian immortality focuses on the annual recurrence of earthly life; Orphic immortality focuses on the periodicity of the heavens from which the individual soul descends: it is preoccupied with the purification and the salvation of the individual soul throughout the round of incarnations. Dionysiac faith has a sense of 'easily and perpetually renewed communion'; Orphism knows dualism, the separation of the bounded and solitary soul in a difficult relation to its others – its body, God, nature, the cosmos. Above all, Orphic immortality of the individual soul has forgotten the Dionysiac knowledge of there being no life without death, 'that there is only one life which dies and is reborn in every shape of existence'.

The untitled preface to *The Space of Literature* directs the reader to the piece entitled 'The Gaze of Orpheus', the centrifuge of the work. *Metaphysically*, Orpheus's turning to gaze at Eurydice is his advent to 'the other death' – not worldly death of rest, silence and end, but death without end, the ordeal of the end's absence, which is the meaning of Eurydice (p. 172). *Existentially*, this piece commends Orpheus's 'mistake' in gazing at Eurydice, that is, to risk everything, to ruin the work, 'to interrupt the incessant by discovering it' (p. 175). It is this sacrifice of the work which makes the work, not as a dialectical gamble, but as the risk that cannot be written without returning to logism, and removing the risk. *For writing*, this experience of 'the other death' can only be approached through art which it consecrates: ruins and makes, 'In this contrarity are situated the essence of writing, the difficulty in the experience and inspiration's leap' (p. 176). This inadvertently captures the meaning of the Holy – beyond contraries and their dialectic. For Blanchot to choose Orphic death as the emblem of 'the other death' is not neutral: it conveys an otherness which is the original separation of the individual soul. Although Orpheus descends into the womb of the earth, and although animals and even trees follow his subsequent song, all seek immortality which, singular and salvific, pertains to the individual soul. If Orphic immortality is to stand for 'the impossibility of dying', ineluctably it bears with it the contours of the separate, solitary, difficult soul, searching for the elixir of life.

'The Original Experience' would seem to deny this individual Orphic immortality by stressing the anonymity and impersonality

of 'the other death' (p. 241). Death as ending, civilisation, achieve-
ment, the risk of the day, is contrasted with the call or command
to lose death as power and possibility, to die 'other than [oneself],
at the level of the neutrality and impersonality of the eternal They'
(pp. 237–42). To embrace a failure which is not no success, but, in
beginning all over again, is 'precisely the *impossibility* of being for
the first time' (p. 243). The work of art begins – not in the worldly
sense of negating to signify or form – but by ruining the kingdom:
'It ruins the origin by returning to it the errant immensity of direc-
tionless eternity' (p. 244). The work is a leap by virtue of its
suspension: 'it hovers between death as the possibility of understanding and death as the horror of impossibility' (p. 244).

Yet the use of existential terms such as 'leap', 'risk', 'ruin' and
'hovering' brings in Orphic connotations of individual salvation.
The image of hovering between the two deaths is comparable to
Kierkegaard's *teleological suspension of the ethical*. In *Fear and
Trembling*, the ethical is bracketed for the sake of the test of faith,
the test of the risk: if the leap is taken then the ethical is
instantaneously resumed – this is the meaning of 'the knight of
faith' who lives the sublime in the pedestrian. If the leap is not
taken because of the preference for infinite pain and resignation,
then the ethical is lost to the suspended soul – this is the meaning
of 'the knight of resignation', who dwells in the romance of the
non-ethical. Blanchot's use of 'hovering' implies suspension in the
sense of *wavering* rather than in the sense of *the return to the
ethical*. This is why he employs contraries whose dialectical relation he must constantly deny: two deaths; not two deaths. There
is no return to the ethical in Blanchot; there is only the endless distress of the poet, who 'dwells in God's default' (p. 246). Yet the
ethical is there or he could not assert that his contraries are not
contraries. Blanchot's double negations display the distraught soul

of loss and resignation, who will not return from 'the other death' to the city or to its work of mourning.

IV

For men it is hard not to look at dead bodies.[7]
Plato, Republic, *Book IV 439e–440e*

Let us look death in the face. In Plato's *Republic* the desire to look at dead bodies lying outside the city wall illustrates the relation of *Thumos*, the principle of high spirit, the third part of the soul, that with which we feel anger, to reason and appetite or desire. Socrates recalls the case of Leontius, son of Aglaion, who could not, as he came up from Piraeus, resist looking at the corpses lying outside the North Wall, the place of public execution. Leontius felt both desire and 'repugnance and aversion, and . . . for a time he resisted and veiled his head, but overpowered . . . by his desire, with wide staring eyes, he rushed up to the corpses and cried [to his eyes] 'There you wretches, take your fill of the fine spectacle'. Socrates and Glaucon confront the dilemma whether the principle of anger (*Thumos*) fights against desire and forms a third to reason and desire, or whether it is indistinguishable from one of them. The case selected for the debate by Socrates involves the most extreme desecration of death in the shameless gaze reported, which occurs, equally, in shame. The gaze arouses the most acute struggle between the three parts of the soul: *Thumos* does not constrain the desire nor aid rational scruple, it accentuates all three to a pitch of internecine warfare. Plato offers this battle within the soul as the analogy of the city – its constitution and its disharmonies.

In 'The Two Versions of the Imaginary', Blanchot contrasts the image as cadaverous remains, 'the absolute neutrality of death',[8] with the image as 'life-giving negation, the ideal operation by which man, capable of negating nature, raises it to signification' (p. 260). The cadaverous 'resemblance' is an image without difference, that is, without an otherness to itself which is self-identity, therefore, 'he resembles *himself*' (p. 258). This is the corpse apart from its being mourned, its being-in-mourning: 'our mourning, the care we take of the dead and *all the prerogatives of our former passions*, since they can no longer know their direction, fall back upon us, return towards us' (p. 257, emphasis added). This response to the cadaver outside mourning is equally without passion; it approaches Stoic *apatheia* – passionlessness – in a world understood as cosmic not political, beyond the warfare within and between cities. 'Eventually we have to put a term to the interminable. We do not cohabit with the dead for fear of seeing *here* collapse into unfathomable *nowhere* . . . And so the dear departed is conveyed into another place'; this 'unsituatable' '*here lies*' is 'the anonymous and impersonal place par excellence' (p. 259).

Between Plato's interested, highest spirit, aroused by the desire to gaze at dead bodies on the boundary of the city, and Blanchot's indifferent, least spirit, drained of passion at the image of the imposing cadaver in unsituatable space, *the disaster* has taken place – the disaster which has made Blanchot vow to renounce all passion, all feeling, all suffering, at the sight of the beloved dead. This leads him to banish the city to the discourse of the *term* – the measure and the monument – yet the term is voided of the difficulty of justice in the city. This 'worldly place' is said to afford a 'level of ambiguity', the third level to the image *qua* power to control things in their absence through fiction and image, and the image *qua* passivity, what he calls 'the passion of indifference'.[9] This passionless gazing at the strange beauty of the dead bodies of those beloved and murdered is *the aberrant mourning*, the mourning *désoeuvré*, of this hymn to death.

V

Banished from the city – in exile, hovering, errant – the law of Blanchot's hymn to death has, however, a name: *the absence of the book*. This absence of the book is introduced by contrast with 'the civilization of the book', and approached via the Bible in which the logos is inscribed as law AND language is taken back to its origin.[10] This would give the idea of the absence of the book a transcendental structure and argument, according to which the absence of the book is 'the prior deterioration of the book . . . with reference to the space in which it is inscribed; the preliminary dying of the book' (p. 151). This disintegrating *a priori* is radicalised so that it does not express a transcendental condition but *a transcendent gnosis of the book* – that is, a transcendence, which is not the contrary of instance nor of immanence, but which, beyond those contraries, is Godhead, white and invisible flame (p. 155), holy and apart writing, from which the demiurgic emanation of the law '*saves us . . . A salvation* that introduces us to knowledge . . .' (p. 158)

This Kabbalistic understanding of the breaking of the first tablets of the law is made explicit: it inaugurates the distinction between the oral Torah and the written Torah, both given to Moses on Sinai in the Rabbinic tradition, which the Kabbalah appropriates antinomically by claiming that the written law itself is an oral commentary on the mystical letters of the original, inaccessible Writing: 'Writing, (pure) exteriority, alien to every relationship of presence and to all legality' (p. 156). Blanchot refers to this Kabbalistic tradition of the invisible writing and its visible interpretation, colourless flame and black fire, by proposing to conduct 'a future experiment of writing' (p. 153), which would tempt us to approach 'an exteriority without limitation', to contact 'otherness itself', 'a severity', 'an austerity', 'the burning of a parching breeze' (pp. 157–8). This theurgic *gnosis*, opposed to the law, which it sees as idolatrous, tempts us to be consumed by the fire of the Godhead.

Blanchot concludes or halts his monumental, interminable *Entretien Infini* with this gnostic transcendence *without the prophets*, this antinomian gaze into divine invisibility *without prophetic justice*. He has presented a mimesis of the *Trauerspiel*, the mourning play, of Jewish exilic history: those periods of expulsion, pogrom and holocaust when even the prophetic justice of the Bible, the portable fatherland, rediscovered whenever the normal insecurities of Rabbinic Jewish life are intensified, can offer no consolation. Under these traumatised conditions, forsaken by the city and in turn forsaking the Torah, Jewish communities have seen the law itself and its traditional commentary as idolatry. In Blanchot, the covenant between God and Israel becomes an unavowable community, for both have succumbed to the disaster.

VI

The disaster ruins everything while leaving everything intact.[11]

Through patience, I take upon myself the relation to the other of the disaster which does not allow me to assume it, nor even to remain myself in order to undergo it. Through patience, all relation between myself and a patient self is lost.[12]

Passivity, the contrary of activity, such is the ever-restricted field of our reflections.[13]

Passivity, 'the hidden face of humanity' (p. 31), advent of, access and response to, the disaster, can be seen as having been prepared philosophically by Blanchot in the long essay in italics which concludes *La Part du Feu* (1949): 'Literature and the Right to Death'. This preparation takes the form of an engagement with activity, consciousness, learning and objectivity in Hegel's *Phenomen-ology of Spirit*. Blanchot sets the engagement in the context of the section of the *Phenomenology* called 'the spiritual-animal kingdom, deceit or the matter in hand [*Das geistige Tierreich und der Betrug oder die Sache selbst*]'. In this section, Hegel expounds the violence of business and affairs when the apparently communal universality of action ('the matter in hand' or 'the thing itself') serves solely ruthless, individual ends, a deception which is not truly ethical but is the way ethical substance is approached and learnt. Blanchot contrasts the meaning of the thing itself (*la chose même*) as 'civilizing power' with the meaning of meaning, 'the absolute concern for truth' which depends on 'an incapacity to act in a real way'.[14] Blanchot's movement from the civil to the absolute may be discerned, therefore, as the movement from the historically structured injustice of the spiritual-animal kingdom to the unworked passivity, sublime and non-sublimated, which is developed in the *Writing of the Disaster*. His *oeuvre* may be shown to be in the grasp of impersonal meanings and powers in a sense which he is unable to acknowledge within his own tran-scendent reduction of the meaning of meaning.

The engagement with Hegel's notion of experience cannot, in effect, take place. In Hegel 'the *disparity* between concept and actuality which lies in [the] essence [of the action of the individ-ual consciousness] is *learnt* by consciousness in its work' (empha-sis added),[15] that is, there is objectivity or objective reality which is learnt by the way in which work as the matter in hand, the thing itself, emerges as *initially* the concern of the individual – her busi-ness or affair – and so deceives others who become involved that they too may participate in it (p. 250). First, deceived, others hurry 'along like flies to freshly-poured milk', only to discover that the individual is concerned with the matter or thing itself, 'not as an *object* but as his own *affair*' (p. 251). Subsequently, all parties learn that they are affected and are invited to participate. It is the coming together of these two experiences that make the thing itself *ethical substance* and the consciousness of it *ethical conscious-ness* (p. 253).

Hegel distinguishes this learning of the actuality and objectivity of ethical substance by means of the work, or the thing itself, from 'the Thing of sense certainty and perception' – the thing which emerged from the sheer negating and distancing power of naming and language. The work 'now acquires its significance through self-consciousness and through it alone; on this rests the distinc-tion between a Thing and a cause or the Thing itself. A movement corresponding to that from [sense-]certainty to perception will run its course here' (p. 246). Blanchot's argument covers *the same two contrasted movements but in reverse order*. Where Hegel moves from naming to action to ethical substance, Blanchot moves from action and the thing itself (*la chose même*) to the name (*la chose*) and its ungraspable remnant, and thence to the absolute meaning of meaning.

Blanchot starts from Hegel's exposition of the work as con-scious action, but he presents *the deception* as the worldliness of the work *per se*,[16] and not as learning the outcome of the originally individual concern when others become involved in it as their work. The work is 'no business but [the writer's] own . . . its indifference mingles hypocritically with everyone's passion' (p. 30). Here the flies have hallucinated the freshly-poured milk acccording to their own, individual affairs. The work is not uni-versal in actuality or deception, it is impersonal – it substitutes the inability to act, the ruin of action in the guise of the negative act of transformation (pp. 35, 36). 'Stoicism', 'scepticism', and the 'unhappy consciousness', which in Hegel stand for various kinds of misrecognition of the work and desire of others thematised as negative relations to 'the world', are here various forms of submission to the unworking of the world which is the work (p. 37). Action remains solely as the temptation to move back from the unreality of the work to realising it; from the space outside history and civilisation to revolutionary action in history (the state, law, etc); to claim the absolute freedom of the Revolution, 'revolutionary action is in every respect analogous to action as embodied in literature' (p. 39).

For Blanchot, the challenge is to move from revolutionary death, described by Hegel as 'the coldest and meanest of all deaths with no more significance than cutting off the head of a cabbage or swallowing a mouthful of water',[17] to the impossibility of dying which is the real dread of man; to move from a frenzy of revolutionary control, through the life which endures death and maintains itself in it,[18] that is, the murder of naming, to the death, 'which does not end anything', the meaning of meaning (p. 58). To effect this movement, Blanchot turns from expounding the work of literature according to the analogy of revolutionary action to the *status* of language itself as naming, to the analogies of destroying 'woman', 'flower', 'Lazarus'. He turns from *the thing itself* to *the thing*:

> When we speak, we gain control over things with satisfying ease. I say, 'This woman,' and she is immediately available to me, I push her away, I bring her close, she is everything I want her to be, she becomes the place in which the most surprising of transformations occur and actions unfold: speech is life's ease and security. We can't do anything with an object that has no name. (p. 41)

To whom is Blanchot speaking? Does she not speak too? She serves the contrast between language as manipulation and words as things (*la chose*), as 'one moment in the universal anonymity'. Nothing, however, can be learnt from the disparity between the evocation of her name and her actuality, *her desire and work*, because she is not a self-relation whose middle term is equally the other's self-relation, his desire and work. The ruin of love, with its always attendant risk of loss, follows from the ruin of action and the impossibility of death in Blanchot. 'Literature and the right to death' yields loveless, endless dying, which remains within the fixed history of the spiritual-animal kingdom, with no disparity and hence no actuality of the spiritual-political kingdom.

VII

However, to watch and to keep awake, over the immeasurable absence, is necessary, it is necessary unceasingly, because what has recommenced from this end (Israel, all of us), is marked by this end from which we will not finish awakening.[19]

The disaster is both 'imminent and immemorial' (p. 39); our access to it demands patience and passivity (p. 14), which 'separate us from all forms of daily activity',[20] AND the disaster is 'the concentration camp, annihilation camp, figures where the invisible is forever made visible'.[21] A third meaning of the disaster is announced, justified, and fixed in this writing: the devastation of knowledge by responsibility.

Concentration camps, annihilation camps, figures where the invisible is forever made visible. All the features of a civilization laid bare . . . The meaning of work [travail] is the destruction of work in and through work/ work ceasing to be [the] manner of living and becoming [the] manner of dying. Knowledge which goes so far as to accept the horrible in order to know it reveals the horror of knowledge, the squalor of coming to know, the discrete complicity which maintains it in a relation with what is insupportable in power. I think of this young prisoner of

Auschwitz (he suffered the worst, led his family to the crematorium, hanged himself; saved – how can one say: saved? – at the last moment – he was exempted from contact with dead bodies, but when the SS shot someone, he was obliged to hold the head of the victim so that the bullet could be more easily lodged in the neck). When asked how he had been able to bear it, he is said to have answered that he 'had observed the bearing of men before death.' I will not believe it. As Lewenthal wrote to us whose notes were found buried near a crematorium: 'The truth was always more atrocious, more tragic than what will be said about it'. Saved at the last instant that young man of whom I speak was every time forced to live and relive, each time frustrated of his own death exchanging it for the death of everyone. His response ('I observed the bearing of men . . .) was not a response; he could not respond. What remains is that, constrained by an impossible question, he could find no other alibi than in the search for knowledge, the claimed dignity of knowledge: that ultimate propriety which we believe will be accorded us by knowledge. And how, in effect, can one accept not to know? We read books on Auschwitz. The wish of all in the camps, the last wish: know what has happened, do not forget, and at the same time, never will you know.

> (*Ibid*., pp. 129–31; trans. pp. 81–2 amended)

I will not believe it. In this passage, knowledge is said to have been offered in the place of response, in place of responsibility. The dignity of knowledge is thereby shown to be obscene. Firstly, Blanchot blames the victim: he should compare the story reconstructed by Christopher Browning of the reserve German policemen, who accepted the commission to shoot Jews, men, women and children, in the neck without any compulsion or prior suffering.[22] Secondly, the statement, 'I observed the bearing of men before death', can be heard as the pathos of an unbearable witness. 'Observing' is the pure passivity which is pure activity; 'the

bearing' is the one moment of possible dignity witnessed *before*
that dying: how the men held themselves, mind and body and soul,
in the face of certain destruction. Thirdly, the last wish of the
victims, 'know what has happened, do not forget, and at the same
time, never will you know', does not command a contradiction,
but it requires a *work*, a working through, that combination of
self-knowledge and action which will not blanch before its
complicities in power – *activity beyond activity*, not passivity
beyond passivity. For power is not necessarily tyranny, but that can
only be discovered by taking the risk of coming to learn it – by
acting, reflecting on the outcome, and then initiating further
action.

What is this response Blanchot would oppose to knowledge?

> Responsible: that qualifies in general . . . the man of action and
> success. But now responsibility – my responsibility for others, for
> everyone, without reciprocity – is displaced, belongs no longer to
> conscience, is not an activating reflection put to work, not even
> a duty which imposes from without and from within. My
> responsibility for the Other presupposes an overturning such
> that it can only be marked by a change in status of me, a change
> in time and perhaps a change in language. Responsibility which
> withdraws me from my order – perhaps from all orders and from
> order itself – and, separating me from myself (from the me that is
> master, power, from the free, speaking subject) discovers the
> other in place of me, requires that I answer for absence, for
> passivity, for the impossibility of being responsible – to which
> this responsibility without measure has already devoted me by
> making me accountable and by discounting me.
>
> (*Ibid.*, pp. 45–6; trans. p. 25 amended)

This paradox destroys the integrity of the subject, subjectivity, the
person, will, resolution, reflective action, and even involuntary
action, any relation of positing (p. 46, trans. pp. 25–6). It exposes

me to 'the passivity without name', by disengaging 'the me from me, the singular from the individual, the subjective from the subject, the non-conscious from the conscious and unconscious' (p. 46, trans. p. 26). 'Declared responsible for dying (for all dying), I can no longer appeal to any ethics, to any experience, to any practice whatsoever', but to '(perhaps) a word of writing . . . in order that this incomprehensible word be understood in its disastrous heaviness without either understanding it or bearing it. That is why responsibility is disastrous – the responsibility never relieves the other (never relieves me of him) and makes us mute of the word which we owe him' (p. 47, trans. p. 27).

This hyperbole amounts to the refusal of the work of mourning – refusal of entering into any experience which *comes to learn* that will, action, reflection and passivity have consequences for others and for oneself which may not be anticipated and can never be completely anticipated; which *comes to learn* its unintended complicity in the use and abuse of power; and hence to redraw, *again and again*, the measures, the bonding and boundaries between me and me, subject and subjectivity, singular and individual, non-conscious and unconscious. This is *activity beyond activity* in three senses: activity emergent from reassessment of the actions of the *initially* abstract person; activity initiated subsequent to the act of imposing *initially* a pure and hence destructive, totalitarian universal. The *work* of these experiences bears the meaning of meaning – the relinquishing *and taking up again* of activity which requires the fullest acknowledgement of active complicity. The work of mourning is difficult but not interminable; beginnings may be made in the middle.

This work of mourning is the spiritual-political kingdom – the difficulty sustained, the transcendence of *actual* justice. Though tyrants rule the city, we understand that we, too, must constantly negotiate the *actuality* of being tyrannical. As I search for the ashes on Potter's Field, as I follow the urgent and haunting voice of our dead from Auschwitz, to know and yet not to know, to be known, to mourn, I incorporate that actual justice in *activity beyond activity*. I would not ruin it forever.

6

O! untimely death. / Death!

O
exclamation mark
untimely death
full stop
new line
Death
exclamation mark

Oswald, King Lear, *Act IV Scene VI lines 247–8*

For Michael Wood

INTRODUCTION

I may die before my time.

Anachronism is customarily taken to mean the retrospective
misplacing of time: attributing to one point in the past the character or conceptuality belonging to some subsequent age, or to concerns which are current. However, if – as we have been
encouraged to generalise – 'anachronism' may be taken to mean

the relation between the time one nominally inhabits and the actuality of any other, then is not *the future* the supreme anachronism?

For the future is the time in which we may not be, and yet we must imagine we will have been. The focus here is not the promiscuous ecstasies of verb-tenses transporting finite being around in time, but *the not*, the time in which we may *not* be. The pathos of syntax, its punctuation, sets time against eternity, the indicative against silence, the determinate against negation.

I may die before my time.

I may *live* before my time

The second reflection overcomes the pusillanimity of the first: the idea of 'living before my time' expands my mind beyond the scale and confines of 'dying before my time'. It makes the lesser or greater bourns of my time within eternity negligible.

When I have fears that I may cease to be

Too early for the ripening grain of my mortality,

I turn to Sir Thomas Browne's *Religio Medici*:

> I am confident, and fully persuaded, yet dare not take the oath of my salvation; I am as it were sure, and do believe, without all doubt, that there is such a City as *Constantinople*, yet for me to take my oath thereon, were a kind of perjury, because I hold no warrant from my owne sense to confirme me in the certainty thereof . . . and suddainely [we unworthy souls] finde how *little* [my emphasis] wee stand in neede of the precept of Saint Paul, *Worke out your salvation with fear and trembling.* That which is the cause of my election, I hold to be the cause of my salvation, which was the mercy, and beneplacit of God, before I was or the foundation of the world. *Before Abraham was, I am,* is the saying of Christ, yet is it true in some sense if I say it of myselfe, for I was not only before myselfe, but *Adam*, that is, in the Idea of God, and the decree of that Synod held from all

> Eternity. And in this sense, I say, the world was before the
> Creation, and at an end before it had a beginning; and thus was I
> dead before I was alive, though my grave be *England*, my dying
> place was Paradise, and *Eve* miscarried me before she conceiv'd
> of *Cain*.   (First Part, para 59, pp. 131–2)

If the 'I' here is *too Protestant*, divinely confident that *no work* needs to be done for his salvation, yet hubristically anxious at the prospect of being carried – it could be miscarried – by that 'I' through eternity, then I propose another occasion for encountering the non-representable thought of eternity in the pathos of its temporal representability.

Without revealing the poet, perhaps I may set the scene, so that you may experience the thrill of learned heterodoxy, as I did and still do. Some years ago, I was wandering in unaccustomed territory, the Oriental shelves in the Norrington Room at Blackwell's bookshop in Oxford, searching for Arberry's versions of Hafiz, the Persian poet, the discovery of whose verse had inspired the aged Goethe, in the thrall of his last great love, to compose the poem-cycle *West-Östlichen Divan*, when I picked off the shelf a sober, brown hardback, with no dust-jacket or author's name, just the enigmatic words engraved on the spine in gold letters: *Divani Shamsi Tabriz*. I opened it at random.

> I was on that day when the Names were not,
>   Nor any sign of existence endowed with name.
> By me Names and Named were brought into view
>   On the day when there was not 'I' and 'We'.
> For a sign, the tip of the Beloved's curl became a centre of
>   revelation;
>   As yet the tip of that fair curl was not.
> Cross and Christians, from end to end,
>   I surveyed; He was not on the Cross.
> I went to the idol-temple, to the ancient pagoda;

No trace was visible there.
I went to the mountains of Herat and Candahar;
I looked; He was not in that hill-and-dale.
                    (*Reynold Nicholson trans.*)

Here the hubris of the eternal 'I' is dissolved in the *viewing* of names and named prior to the division between 'I' and 'We'. Yet division and separation are the agony of the poem, the eros of the Beloved's curl, the absolute revelation which is, simultaneously, the absolute loss of the Beloved: Shams Tabriz. The juxtaposition of curl and cross equalises the Greek and Hebrew traditions. The arrogant Aristotelian I, divested of its intellectual activity, becomes embroiled in the search among the holy places and the holy names of orthodox securities, which are sequentially disqualified.

However, the accumulated negations ('when the names were not'; 'there were not 'I' and 'We'; 'the tip of that fair curl was not'; 'not on the Cross'; 'no trace'; 'not in that hill-and-dale') ensure that *the nots are not nothing*: that the silence of Tabriz's disappearance is articulated in its determinations. In this way, divine and human transcendence can be represented. Erotic and religious absence are invoked by a poetic voice which has also staked itself on the confidence justified by names (Constantinople, curl, Cross, Candahar), by human love, and by the monotheistic and pagan faiths, whose no longer warring symbolisms yield the Lover's energy for time and for eternity.

In this first of two stanzas, the disappearance and death of Shams Tabriz, before his time to the grieving eyes of the Lover, are held in the eternity before the time of either Lover or Beloved. This is not to deny grief in elegy, not to suspend or to colonise death or suffering, not to achieve any consolation, but to emphasise the experience of death in the times and in the eternity of its determinate actuality.

Where there is nothing, there is God

I may die before my time

'Before my time' – *my time*? How can I claim to *own* a time when death is nothing? Since if death is nothing, then life is nothing, for the idea of death cannot confer the significance of its limit on life. The time which is calibrated by that shared limit loses its vitality.

I cannot live, if death be nought, but neither can I die if life be not aught.

This is the nonfatal logic which follows from the disguised Duke's exhortation to Claudio, who is under sentence of death, in *Measure for Measure*: 'Be absolute for death' (Act III, scene i). The Duke's oration, in his disguise of a friar, voids life of all value, with the result that Claudio becomes even less capable of resolving to leave it.

> This inability to die has become the work of philosophy.
> For philosophy cannot let death go free;
> And so it robs us both of our time and of our eternity.
> Instead we have the death of philosophy.

I dub three versions of this:

1 Modern Life and Modern Death
2 Freedom of Finitude
3 Death by Determination

MODERN LIFE AND MODERN DEATH FROM TOLSTOY TO TRAUERSPIEL

In Max Weber's essay 'Science as a Vocation' (one of the twin, magnificent, inexhaustible essays from 1919. I shall discuss the other one, 'Politics as a Vocation' later), Weber outlines Tolstoy's

response to the question whether death is a meaningful phenom-
enon as 'the most principled form' of pursuing the Occidental, mil-
lenial 'process of disenchantment'.

And his answer was: for civilised man death has no meaning. It
has none because the individual life of civilised man, placed into
an infinite 'progress', according to its immanent meaning should
never come to an end; for there is always a further step ahead of
one who stands in the march of progress. And no man who comes
to die stands upon the peak which lies in infinity. Abraham, or
some peasant of the past, died 'old and satiated with life' because
he stood in the organic cycle of life; because his life, in terms of its
meaning and on the eve of its days, had given to him what life had
to offer; because for him there remained no more puzzles he might
wish to solve; and therefore he could have had 'enough' of life.
Whereas civilised man, placed in the midst of the continuous
enrichment of culture by ideas, knowledge, and problems, may
become 'tired of life' but not 'satiated with life'. He catches only
the most minute part of what the life of the spirit brings forth ever
anew, and what he seizes is always something provisional and not
definitive, and therefore death for him is a meaningless occurrence. And because death is meaningless, life itself is meaningless;
by its very 'progressiveness' it gives death the imprint of meaning-
lessness. Throughout his late novels one meets with this thought
as the keynote of the Tolstoyan art (*From Max Weber*, pp. 139–40).

The implicit keynote here is not the commonplace regarding the
general loss of faith, but loss of faith in the eternal, as opposed to
faith in the incessant, infinitesimal movement of finite knowledge.
While *the rationalisation of life*, the process of disenchantment,
is attributed to the West and its civilisation, its details are taken
from the modern notion of scientific progress. If this argument
captures the aspiration of enlightenment, then the destructive

potential of modern science, *the rationalisation of death* in modern warfare and genocide, is often cited as the complementary devastation of the traditionally meaningful experience of death.

Although Walter Benjamin traces the degeneration of experience in the ruined tradition of the story-teller, and elsewhere, his most ambitious attempt at philosophical description of unredeemable death occurs in the *Origin of German Trauerspiel.* This formidable account of the seventeenth-century baroque mourning play constitutes a study of *the political ethic* of the Protestant Counter-Reformation. It provides, too, the underpinning for Benjamin's exploration of the political psychology of fascism.

> The baroque knows no eschatology . . . no mechanism by which all earthly things are gathered in together and exalted before being consigned to their end. The hereafter is emptied of everything which contains the slightest breath of this world, and from it the baroque extracts a profusion of things which customarily escaped the grasp of artistic formulation and, at its high point, brings them violently into the light of day, in order to clear an ultimate heaven, enabling it, as a vacuum, one day to destroy the world with catastrophic violence.   (trans. p. 66)

I know no passage which deals so profoundly with the violent implications of the nothingness of death. If all things retain in death their weight without soul, if death does not mean the passage to the eternal, not even eternal damnation, then the Other itself can only be indiscriminate and absolute catastrophe: the God at whose approach everything shrivels up; the God who has cancelled the revelation effected by his partial withdrawal, which gave creation the freedom to err. This God is non-determinate Otherness, non-ontic or beyond ontology; and death is nothing, endless in its extermination of life.

Whereas in the symbol destruction is idealised and the transfigured face of nature fleetingly revealed in the light of redemption, in allegory the observer is confronted with the *facies hippocratica* of history as a petrified, primordial landscape. Everything about history that, from the very beginning, has been untimely, sorrowful, unsuccessful, is expressed in a face – or rather in a death's head. This is the heart of the allegorical way of seeing, of the baroque, secular explanation of history as the Passion of the world; its importance resides solely in the stations of its decline.

(trans. p. 166)

We cannot speak without spirit, without, that is, taking up a relation to the relation, to the ensouling of things when they become meaning. When we speak of death, which is the demarcation between physical nature and signification, we take up a relation to the relation of body and soul, their salvation or damnation. The vista of death without redemption or doom, of death as the utter abjection of things, acquires representation in allegory. Death as nothing is pure violence beyond representation; yet in allegory that death without soul is taken up into spirit. It can thus be witnessed, even if only in the repetition of its nothingness. If death is nothing, then this death and this nothing have a history – call it baroque, call it fascism.

These paradoxes are parallel to that of Duke Vincentio: contrary to his intention to preach absoluteness for death, he paints a death that cannot die, because it depends on the total degradation of life. Life and death become indistinguishable, for nature is depicted as the death's face or head, not as the fleeting but transfigured face of eternity. Death is therefore nothing. Yet *something* is spiritualised in the very art of oratory.

FREEDOM OF FINITUDE FROM
HEIDEGGER TO BLANCHOT

With the existential version of death as nothing, death becomes *transcendental without transcendence*. The violence of this God of nothingness, this Otherness without determination, emerges here, too.

Levinas rightly corrects Jean Wahl in a footnote to *Time and the Other*: 'Death in Heidegger is not . . . "the impossibility of possibility", but "the possibility of impossibility".' He then adds, 'This apparently Byzantine distinction has a fundamental importance.' While the distinction which Levinas draws is crucial to differentiating his position on death from Heidegger's, it turns out to be, however, a distinction without a difference (*op. cit.* trans. p. 70 n. 43).

For if the nothingness of death is presented in Heidegger as 'the possibility of impossibility', and in Levinas as 'the impossibility of possibility', and in Blanchot as two deaths, one possible, the other impossible, then all three accounts attribute a pseudo-Kantian hermeneutic circle to the nothingness of death: where nothing as possible or as impossible becomes the condition of all possible experience – experience which is therefore nugatory.

According to Levinas, death in Heidegger is a possible nothingness, whereas, for Levinas, it is 'the call to an impossible nothingness, the proximity of death'. For Heidegger, being-towards-death 'is a supreme lucidity and hence a supreme virility,' whereas for Levinas, the proximity of death is 'foreign to all light', 'absolutely unknowable' and deprives the subject of mastery. For Heidegger, the nothingness of death permits Dasein's 'assumption of the uttermost possibility of existence which precisely makes possible all other possibilities'; for Levinas, while assumption of possibility may occur as an heroic last chance, 'death is never assumed, it comes'. For Heidegger, the nothingness of death founds human freedom, for Levinas, it devastates human freedom, by making us 'no longer *able to be able*'. The relationship with this other, this mystery, 'will never be the feat of grasping a possibility'. For Levinas, possibility presupposes light, vision, graspability and knowability. Hence 'Nothingness is impossibility' (*ibid.*, pp. 70–3). Anxiety in face of the nothingness of death in Heidegger, becomes in Levinas, 'fear of violence of the Other, of the absolutely unforeseeable' (*Totality and Infinity*, trans., p. 235).

The adequacy of the contrasts drawn by Levinas between his position and Heidegger's is not the issue here. What is important is what these two accounts have in common. Levinas, in spite of the contrast between the foundational nature of Heidegger's *being-towards-death* and his own account as non-foundational, has produced a foundational account. For if 'freedom' is derived from Dasein's assumption of possibility in the anticipation of death, so 'passivity beyond passivity' is derived from Levinas's *proximity of death*. In both cases, ethical actuality is established by what is possible or impossible. Both accounts strive to present the fate of finitude. The definition of death as 'the possibility of nothing', or as 'the impossibility of nothing', presuppose a being with no inner relation to the meaning of death, a being whose finitude is in no determinate relation to transcendence. In Levinas, the impossibility of nothing is the name of the absolutely Other conceived as violence or threat. The relation with that infinite but not eternal Other is presented as beyond possibility or knowledge, as depending on a will without egoism, need or efficacy (a very Protestant will!) (*ibid.*, pp. 245–6). Finally, what the two accounts have in common is the pivot of assumability: the nothingness of death as what requires possibility to be assumed, or forces its divestiture.

This is the pivot of comparability with Blanchot, who splits the
nothing of death in two: the death which is possible and the death
which is impossible, the one assumable, the other not assumable,
the night which turns into day and the endless night, the death
which interrupts time and the endless, but not eternal, death:
'death's space'. For Blanchot, Rilke's poetry is the supreme
witness, 'the work', of this *space*, as Shakespeare is the supreme
witness for Levinas ('it seems to me that the whole of philosophy
is only a meditation of Shakespeare': *Time and the Other*, p. 72. I
find this confounding given Levinas's complete lack of interest in
political virtue.).

Blanchot attributes 'the decision to be without being', that is, in
relation to the nothing of death, to 'possibility itself' (*Space of
Literature*, trans. p. 96). Hegel, Heidegger and Nietzsche 'are all
attempts at making death possible'. Like Levinas, Blanchot sees
this death as mastery, as turned towards life and mind, and away
from the abyss: it affirms resolution and certitude. But 'the other
death' 'dwells with negation' and so 'cannot use it'; it has no certainty, 'disorients every project, remains foreign to all decision'. 'It
is what I cannot grasp, what is not linked to me by any relation of
any sort'. One death is the continuation of power (that is, after all,
the meaning of 'possibility'); *the other death* is the radical reversal of that power. 'I cannot represent this reversal to myself . . . It
is not the irreversible step beyond which there would be no return,
for it is that which is not accomplished, the interminable and the
incessant' – the *désoeuvré* (*ibid.*, pp. 100–6).

Poetry 'wants, so to speak, to install itself, to dwell in this *neg-
ligence*' (*ibid.*, p. 107). It places itself (space not time is the metaphor here) at the ordeal, the risk stake of the reversal from the
one nothing to the other nothing, and sings, sings to Orpheus.
The reversal, from what Blanchot also calls 'personal death' to

'impersonal' death, can be traced in Rilke's poetry from the prayer for a monumental death, a death which can be commemorated, which is the meaning of my life and which I have brought to fruition, in *Malte Laurids Brigge*:

> Oh Lord, grant to each his own death, the dying which truly
> evolves from this life where he found love, meaning and distress

to the death in the *Elegies* and *Sonnets* which is not mine, and which Blanchot puts into the form of a comparable prayer: 'grant me the death of no-one, the dying which truly evolves from death, where I am not called up to die, which is not an event that would be proper to me, which would happen to me alone – but the unreality and absence where nothing happens, where neither love nor meaning nor distress accompanies me, but the pure abandon of all that' (*ibid.*, p. 149).

For Blanchot, this other death is what Rilke sings as 'the pure relation': It 'is the purity of the relation: the fact of being, in this relation, outside oneself, in the thing itself, and not in a representation of the thing' (*ibid.*, p. 135).

In order to convey that the contrary of life and death is unlike other contraries because all other contraries posit *something*, whereas death is nothing, the contrary of contraries, the negation of all experience, all three thinkers employ further sets of non-analogous contraries: light/dark, mastery/passivity, possibility/impossibility, assumable/unassumable. All these contraries serve to keep death as the negation of contraries as such, hence as nothing, without determination, the *violation* of all determination.

Can this be so? Does not the idea of whatever cannot be assumed draw on the richness of our reversals? Of familiar experience as reversal? Do we *assume* sleep, dreams, laughter, rage, sadness? *In sooth I know not why I am so sad.* Do we *assume* the moment looking out from the train, when the bare, charcoal landscape heaves a deep sigh, and takes on the hazy hues of brown? Is all knowing *mastery*, and not rather *attention*, the natural prayer of the soul? Are there not determinate ways of thinking or singing which convey our reversals without the anti-metaphysics of nothing? The contortions of philosophical discourse in Heidegger, Levinas and Blanchot arise from their attempts to elude the eternity of syntax, the passage from nature to eternity which is the passage through the human spirit:

> To understand that, humanly, it is his destruction, and then
> nevertheless to believe in the possibility, is what is meant by faith
> . . . Therefore he does not succumb   (p. 72)

In *The Sickness unto Death* Kierkegaard writes under the pseudonym of 'Anti-Climacus' so that we should not view the Name instead of our own exposure. 'Possibility' here is transcendent not transcendental; the destruction 'in what has befallen him and in what he has ventured' in death, calls for a trust without security. It does not make experience meaningless. The transcendence of the negation preserves all determinations; it does not mark them with the transcendental death's head.

DEATH BY DETERMINATION

Both versions of death as nothing, *Trauerspiel*, mourning play, where there is no mourning, and finite death of existential freedom or passivity, present death without determination and presuppose life without reason, or with demonic reason. These presentations of individual life and death without salvation or eternity (for Levinas's 'infinity' and Blanchot's 'endlessness' are not *eternity*) claim that they acknowledge uniquely the Otherness of death.

They claim thereby to overturn the metaphysical tradition, which – in an extreme statement – has amounted to 'the obscene colonising of death' (Bataille on Hegel). Self-consciousness is said to return Otherness to itself by representation, idealisation and assimilation. The rupture of Otherness is mended, routinised and categorised.

In Kierkegaard's pseudonymous *Philosophical Fragments*, determinate negation in Hegel's thought – that out of experience, however negative, something emerges – is presented as a determinist historicism, as a logic according to which everything that happens *had* to happen. This *panlogism* is opposed to the *crisis of Christ*, the irruption of the eternal as scandal into the continuities of historical experience. However, this is an argument between *two views of eternity*: a triune or trinitarian exposition of experience as recognition in Hegel, and the incursion or crisis of faith in Kierkegaard's pseudonymous, philosophical authorship, which, nevertheless, in his directly Christian works, is also trinitarian.

According to death by determination, the argument is between the metaphysical tradition, which is said to have killed death by denial of its radical Otherness to the concept, that is, by determining it, and existential nihilism which can itself only confront death as nothing by contrast to the positings of finite being. According to the existentialist view, these vain positings constitute life.

> To rob life, death and language of their eternity
> Does not let death go free;
> It constricts it to mere vacuity.
> Determinate negation holds the reversal
> And thus lets it go –
> Death ceases to be

O! untimely death. / Death!

> Solipsistic self-elegy;
> It pertains to a life
> That has been able to grow.

Well, what could be the determinations of death?

RHETORIC AND VIRTUE

> I may die before my time.
> Die at the right time!
> Who is commanding me?
> Zarathustra!

Zarathustra continues: 'To be sure, he who never lived at the right time could hardly die at the right time! Better if he were never to be born! – Thus I advise the superfluous' ('Of Voluntary Death', p. 97).

What does this commandment command? Is it, as Blanchot claims, just another, albeit dramatised, foundational discourse? Does it just employ the rhetoric of commandment to revitalise the tired commonplace that living well is the precondition of dying well, that the nothingness of death is life's possibility? This cannot be: for it assimilates Zarathustra to Nietzsche and then to a Kantian psychology and morality: a possibility or faculty to live and a categorical commandment. But Zarathustra proclaims, 'Only where life is, there is also will: not will to life, but – so I teach you – will to power!' Zarathustra teaches us that we value power not life *per se*, and that we act out of the predicament of will to power, not by power to will, not by exercising the faculty or possibility of the will ('Of Self-Overcoming', p. 138).

Do we have here, then, the ultimate nihilistic injunction to die by suicide? 'I commend to you my sort of death, voluntary death that comes to me because *I* wish it!' (*ibid.*, p. 97) To reduce the notion of 'voluntary death' to suicide, self-destruction, is to fail to hear the affirmation of the will in the idea of the voluntary, which may prevail in any 'natural' death. And lest this sound too voluntaristic, it is also to fail to heed the political and religious polemic which gives the idea of voluntary death its determination: Christian death. I say 'polemic' for Nietzsche dramatises the authorial voice as the agon of a man of *ressentiment* with a free spirit, a noble man. The new nobility can only issue from the cunning and creativity of *ressentiment* as a culture. This histrionic representation I take to be *the meaning of genealogy as a method.* (See 'Nietzsche's Judaica' in *Judaism and Modernity*.)

From 'Skirmishes' in *Twilight of the Idols*:

> To die proudly when it is no longer possible to live proudly.
> Death of one's own free choice, death at the proper time; with a
> clear head and with joyfulness, consummated in the midst of
> children and witnesses: so that an actual leave-taking is possible
> while he who is living *is still there*, likewise an actual evaluation
> of what has been desired and what achieved in life, an *adding
> up* of life – all of this in contrast to the pitiable and horrible
> comedy Christianity has made of death. One should never forget
> of Christianity that it has abused the weakness of the dying to
> commit conscience-rape and even the mode of death to
> formulate value judgements on men and the past!
>
> (sect. 36, p. 88)

The proud death recommended here is the death that has taken up the challenge of will to power, of the free spirit, of true nobility, of virtue. Against MacIntyre who, in *After Virtue*, opposes Aristotelian ethics to Nietzschean nihilism and amoralism, I argue that the three great thinkers of *power before ethics*, Machiavelli, Nietzsche and Weber, each renew the classical tradition in ethics for the modern world. In opposition to Christian eschatology, negotiating the dilemma of power and violence becomes the pre-

condition for configuring virtue for the modern polity. The virtuous life involves some *impure* relation between power in the
human psyche and in human association. Against *the purity of
politics* imagined in Arendt's Augustinian constituting of liberty,
and in current versions of communitarian and neo-liberal politics,
the impure paradoxes of the disposition of power renew virtue in
life and in death. To know the violence at the heart of the human
spirit gives death back its determination and its eternity.

In all his works, Nietzsche explores the meaning of nobility in
opposition to, and, equally, in appropriation of, Christian, especially Protestant, ignobility, *ressentiment* and cunning. Compare
Machiavelli's argument from the *Discourses*, Book 2, chapter 2,
6–7 with the second essay in the *Genealogy of Morals*:

> If one asks oneself how it comes about that peoples of old were
> more fond of liberty than they are today, I think the answer is
> that it is due to the same cause that makes men today less bold
> than they used to be; and this is due, I think, to the difference
> between our religion and the religion of those days. For our
> religion, having taught us the truth and the true way of life, leads
> us to ascribe less esteem to worldly honour. Hence the gentiles,
> who held it in high esteem and looked upon it as their highest
> good, displayed in their actions more ferocity than we do. This is
> evidenced by many of their institutions. To begin with, compare
> the magnificence of their sacrifices with the humility that
> characterises ours. The ceremonial in ours is delicate rather than
> imposing, and there is no display of ferocity or courage. Their
> ceremonies lacked neither pomp or magnificence, but, conjoined
> with this, were sacrificial acts in which there was much shedding
> of blood and much ferocity; and in them great numbers of
> animals were killed. Such spectacles, because terrible, caused
> men to become like them. Besides, the old religion did not
> beatify men unless they were replete with worldly glory: army
> commanders, for instance, and rulers of republics. Our religion

has glorified humble and contemplative men, rather than men of action.It has assigned as man's highest good humility, abnegation, and contempt for mundane things, whereas the other identifies it with magnanimity, bodily strength, and everything else that tends to make men very bold. And if our religion demands that in you there be strength, what it asks for is strength to suffer rather than the strength to do bold things.

Machiavelli compares two kinds of death in two kinds of ceremonial: one replete with worldly glory, based on bold and courageous deeds, the other impoverished by withdrawal from the world, and contempt for mundane things. The one ceremony celebrates, in the killing of animals, the violence out of which virtue emerges; the other substitutes a delicacy in which the human will is sacrificed. In the context of Machiavelli's thought in general I find this striking passage strange: it reads like a critique of Protestantism to come. For in his *Florentine Histories*, Machiavelli sees the Pope as a secular Prince among Princes, if anything more worldly in pomp and ferocity than the other Italian Princes and Republics.

In Nietzsche and Weber the opposition to Christianity is typically based on the characterisation of Protestant Christianity: the mix of abnegation of the human will, its total inefficacy in the work of salvation, together with the authoritarian state and ruthless exploitation of the world. In his second essay from 1919 'Politics as a Vocation', Weber appropriates Machiavelli to his own emphasis on human association or *politics* as the *means* of legitimate violence. Nevertheless, Weber is interested in true statesmanship, the stake in the *end* of *politics*. Statesmanship requires vigilance to ethical paradoxes, to the 'diabolic forces lurking in violence' ('Politics as a Vocation', pp. 125–6). While these forces attend both the ethic of responsibility and the ethic of ultimate ends, the ethic of ultimate ends is potentially more destructive, whether it causes politics to be abandoned and therefore exposes others to power, or whether it espouses politics and violence as the means to its non-violent end. Still, Weber also endorses the opposition of Christian eschatology to political virtue found in Machiavelli and Nietzsche:

> He who seeks salvation of his soul, of his own and of others, should not seek it along the avenue of politics, for the quite different tasks of politics can only be solved by violence. The genius or demon of politics lives in an inner tension with the god of love, as well as with the Christian God as expressed by the Church. This tension can at any time lead to an irreconcilable conflict. Men knew this even in the time of Church rule. Time and again the papal interdict was placed on Florence and at the time it meant a far more robust power for men and their salvation of soul than (to speak with Fichte) the 'cool approbation of the Kantian ethical judgement'. The burghers, however, fought the church-state. And it is with reference to such situations that Machiavelli in a beautiful passage, if I am not mistaken, of the *History of Florence*, has one of his heroes praise those citizens who deemed the greatness of the native city higher than the salvation of their souls.
>
> (*Ibid.*, p. 126)

Weber may have conflated the censure of Pope Gregory XI, when 'so much more did these citizens then esteem their fatherland than their souls' (III:7), with the reconstruction of Lorenzo de Medici's speech to the citizens, when Florence lay again under a papal interdict (VIII:10–11).

However, like Machiavelli and Nietzsche, Weber proceeds to weave the ethic of salvation into the ethics of responsibility to produce his final definition of a mature 'calling for politics'. He restores spiritual meaning, virtue, to politics as the means of violence. His animus is reserved for the Protestant combination of an acosmic, world-denying ethic with the *absolute* legitimation of the state as a divine institution and violence as a means, so that 'to obey the authorities in matters other than faith could never constitute guilt' (*ibid.*, p. 124).

Noble politics in all three, Machiavelli, Nietzsche and Weber, then, is 'a bridge to love', as Nietzsche concludes regarding honouring and not hating your enemy in *On the Genealogy of Morals* (First Essay, sect. 10).

> To be incapable of taking one's enemies, one's accidents, even
> one's misdeeds seriously for very long – that is a sign of strong,
> full natures in whom there is an excess of the power to form, to
> mold, to recuperate and to forget . . . Such a man shakes off with
> a *single* shrug much vermin that eats deep into others; here
> alone genuine 'love of one's enemies' is possible – supposing it to
> be possible at all on earth. How much reverence has a noble
> man for his enemies! – and such reverence is a bridge to love. –
> For he desires his enemy for himself, as his mark of distinction;
> he can endure no other enemy than one in whom there is
> nothing to despise and *very much* to honor! In contrast to this,
> picture 'the enemy' as the man of *ressentiment* conceives him –
> and here precisely is his deed, his creation: he has conceived 'the
> evil enemy', '*the Evil One*', and this in fact is his basic concept,
> from which he then evolves, as an afterthought and pendant, a
> 'good one' – himself!
>
> (Trans. Walter Kaufmann, New York, 1969)

In this vigilance to violence in its toils with virtue, reason is crying: reason sheds *uncontrollable* tears at the pain of rearranging its resources; at the pain of enlarging as well as curtailing its limits.

Proud death then becomes a bridge to true humility.

SYNTAX AND ETERNITY

The rhetoric of the commandment reveals the interest in virtue: from the disguised Duke, 'Be absolute for death' to Zarathustra,

'Die at the right time' to the Orphic imperative, 'Be ever dead in Eurydice – arise singing with greater praise, rise again to the pure relation.' These categorical imperatives issue from the masks of Prince, Prophet, Mystagogue: the Duke, Zarathustra, Orpheus. They do not transform the nothing of death into possibility; but nor do they allude to that nothing as the impersonality of death, 'the pure relation'. The *poignancy* of their perfectionism is the pathos of eternity in the implied repetition of the commandment itself.

> Be ahead of all departure, as if it were behind
>   you, like the winter that is just now passed.
> In winters you are so endlessly winter, you find
>   that, getting through winter, your heart on the whole will last.
>
> Be ever dead in Eurydice – arise singing
>   with greater praise, rise again to the pure relation.
> Here among the fleeting, be, in the realm of declination,
>   be a resonant glass that shatters while it is ringing.
>
> Be – and at the same time, know the terms of negation,
>   the infinite basis of your fervent vibration,
>   that you may completely complete it this one time.
>
> To teeming nature's store of used, as of dumb
>   and moldy things, to that uncountable count,
>   add yourself joyously, and annul the amount.
> Sonnets to Orpheus, Part Two, 13 *(C.F. MacIntyre trans. (amended))*

This appeal holds out no impersonal, endless dying, but eternity, 'Be *ever* dead in Eurydice.' The rise to the pure relation is the call not to lamentation, but to praise, to magnify the eternal in the fleeting, in the speechless declination of nature's realm. Retrospectively, our ability to survive the difficulties of winter is introduced as the model and analogy for all anticipatable loss. To be ahead of all departure must surely require the most excruciating practice of anachronism. The opening verse bears the syntax of determinate negation: it calls on our *endurance* of the negative and, hence, its movement. The crescendo of active affirmation of eternity in 'be ever dead in Eurydice' places the nihilistic moment of shattering glass in determination, for it rings and resounds. *Endurance* and *eternity* meet in this instant, and they issue in the further command, now warranted: 'Be – and at the same time know the terms of negation.' This knowledge does not fall into the opposition of mastery/passivity: it acknowledges the negative as it moves beyond eternal loss to eternal confirmation, and adds itself, without count, to the teeming mass of natural declining determinations.

The rhetoric of virtue, virtue alive to the negative, is discernible in the pathos of syntax, where eternity shines through violence, where transcendence percolates immanence.

This death is not nothing.

I may die before my time.

The Saints are ever failing from the earth and Christ is all but coming.

Without commandment or simple negation, the syntax of this surely heterodox and humorous aphorism from John Henry Newman celebrates the absence-presence of the eternal in figuration – both verbal and earthy.

The falconer is ever failing from the falcons, the Second Bethlehem is all but coming.

Paradise is ever failing from the earth and the wasps are but all coming.

Thanks to Nabokov for that last little inversion of 'all but'.

What time occurs between this 'ever failing' and this 'all but coming'?

My time and yours,

Time to praise all others –

Placeable and unplaceable time

NOTES

I ATHENS AND JERUSALEM

A version of this chapter was first delivered as the author's Inaugural Lecture at the University of Warwick, 15 February 1993. It was first published in *Social and Legal Studies*, vol. 3, 1994, 338–48.

2 BEGINNINGS OF THE DAY

This chapter was first prepared for the conference 'Modernity, Culture and "the Jew"', Birkbeck College, University of London, May 1994.

1 See Shoshana Felman 'The Return of the Voice: Claude Lanzmann's *Shoah*', in Felman and Laub (eds.), *Testimony: Crises of Witnessing in Literature, Psychoanalysis and History*, 1992.

3 THE COMEDY OF HEGEL

This chapter was originally prepared for the conference 'Modernism: Politics, Poetics, Practice', King's College, Cambridge, July 1993. A version was first published in *Bulletin of the Hegel Society of Great Britain*, no. 29, Spring/Summer 1994, 14–22.

1 *Aesthetics: Lectures on Fine Art*, trans. T. M. Knox, Oxford, The Clarendon Press, vol. 2 trans. amended.

2 I refer here to Nietzsche's argument that '*complete nihilism* is the necessary consequence of the ideals entertained hitherto'; it involves the active transvaluating of values as opposed to passive and incomplete nihilism, 'its forms: we live in the midst of it.' (See *The Will to Power*,

trans. Walter Kaufmann and R. J. Hollingdale, New York, Vintage, 1968, Book I: *European Nihilism*, sects. 22, 28).

3 I employ here Freud's distinction between 'Mourning and Melancholia' (see *The Penguin Freud Library*, vol.11, *On Metapsychology*, Harmondsworth, 1984, pp. 245–68.)

4 For *aberrated mourning*, see Laurence A. Rickels, *Aberrations of Mourning: Writing on German Crypts*, Detroit, Wayne State University Press, 1988; for *inaugurated mourning*, compare the inaugurated eschatology of John Climacus, *The Ladder of Divine Ascent*, trans. Colm Luibheid and Norman Russell, London, SPCK, 1982.

5 Now published as a book (1993), trans. Peggy Kanuf, London, Routledge, 1994

6 This subsequently became the opening essay of *History and Class Consciousness: Studies in Marxist Dialectics* (1923), trans. Rodney Livingstone, London, Merlin, 1971, pp. 1–26.

7 See *Of Spirit: Heidegger and the Question*, trans. Geoffrey Bennington and Rachel Bowlby, Chicago, Chicago University Press, 1989.

8 *Capital* vol. 1, trans. Harmondsworth, Penguin 1976, p. 72.

9 *Ibid.*, p. 107.

10 See 'Force of Law: The "Mystical Foundation of Authority"', in *Cardozo Law Review*, 'Deconstruction and the Possibility of Justice' (vol. 11, July–Aug. 1990, nos. 5–6) 919–1045.

11 *Ibid.*, pp. 919–73.

12 'Theses on the Philosophy of History' (1940), in *Illuminations*, trans. Harry Zohn, London, Collins, 1973, pp. 255–66.

13 *Cardozo Law Review*, vol. 11, 1990, 973–1039.

14 *The Origin of German Tragic Drama* (1928), trans. John Osborne, London, New Left Books, 1977.

15 *Glas* remains Derrida's most sustained engagement with Hegel's thought, but not from the perspective of the relation between Marx and the Hegelian dialectic (see *Glas* (1974), trans. John P. Leavey, Jr, and Richard Rand, Lincoln, University of Nebraska Press, 1986).

16 See Hegel, *Aesthetics*, vol. 11, pp1234–6.

4 MIDRASH AND POLITICAL AUTHORITY

This paper was first presented at the conference 'Culture and Critical Form: Reading After Geoffrey Hartman', 8–9 May 1993, University of Warwick. I would like to thank Peter Larkin for the opportunity of presenting this paper and for providing much relevant material; and Rowland Cotterill for delivering the paper, for correcting it, and for much support. Thanks to Vassilic Lambropoulos for helping me formulate the Preface. The title quote is drawn from *Jerusalem Talmud, Haggigah* 1:7. The paper was subsequently published in *The Modern Law Review*, Vol. 58, No. 4 (1995) and is reproduced by permission.

1 *The Rise of Eurocentricism*, Princeton, Princeton University Press, 1993, pp. 86–96, 260.
2 Harold Bloom, *The American Religion: The Emergence of the Post-Christian Nation*, New York, Simon and Schuster, 1992.
3 Martin Bernal, *Black Athena, The Afroasiatic Roots of of Classical Civilization*, London, Vintage, 1987, 1991
4 *Ibid.*, pp. 88, 206–7, 319–20.
5 *Ibid.*, p. 207.
6 *Ibid.*, p. 101.
7 'Religious Literacy', in *Conservative Judaism*, vol. 40, no. 4, Summer 1988, 26–34.
8 *The Yale Review*, 51, 52, 53.
9 *Ibid.*, 58–9.
10 'Religious Literacy', 32.
11 'Art and Consensus in the Era of Progressive Politics', p. 61; 'Religious Literacy', pp. 30, 26.
12 'Jewish Hermeneutics and Contemporary Theories of Textuality: Hartman, Bloom, and Derrida', *Modern Philology*, Vol. 85:1 (August 1987), 65–80.
13 'Religious Literacy', p. 29.
14 *Ibid.*, p. 32.
15 Cited by Mortimer Ostow in 'Four Entered the Garden: Normative Religion versus Illusion', in *Conservative Judaism*, vol.40, no. 4, Summer 1988, 35.
16 See Louis Finkelstein, *Akiba: Scholar, Saint and Martyr* (1936), New York, Atheneum, 1985.
17 *The Star of Redemption* (1921), trans. William W. Hallo, London, Routledge and Kegan Paul, 1971, p. 331.
18 *Economy and Society: An Outline of Interpretative Sociology*, ed. Guenther Roth and Claus Withich, 2 vols. Berkeley, University of California Press, 1978
19 J. G. A. Pocock, *The Machiavellian Moment: Florentine Political Thought and the Atlantic Republican Tradition*, Princeton, Princeton University Press, 1975.

20 *Ibid.*, p. 157.

21 See Hermann L. Strack, *Introduction to The Talmud and Midrash*, Philadelphia, The Jewish Publication Society of America, 1945.

22 See Jacob Neusner, *Rabbinic Political Theory: Religion and Politics in the Mishnah*, Chicago, University of Chicago Press, 1991, p. 14.

23 See Daniel J. Elazar and Stuart A. Cohen, *The Jewish Polity: Jewish Political Organization from the Biblical Times to the Present*, Bloomington, Indiana University Press, 1984.

24 Stuart A. Cohen, *The Three Crowns: Structures of Communal Politics in Early Rabbinic Jewry*, Cambridge, Cambridge University Press, 1990, pp. 8–10.

25 *Ibid.*, p. 72. See, too, Neusner, *Rabbinic Political Theory*, chapter 3, pp. 39–57.

26 Elazar and Cohen, *The Jewish Polity*, pp. 109,112, 197.

27 *Ibid.*, pp. 258–303.

28 See Neusner, *Judaism and its Social Metaphors: Israel in the History of Jewish Thought*, Cambridge, Cambridge University Press, 1989.

29 See Simon Schwarzfuchs, *Napoleon, the Jews and the Sanhedrin*, London, Routledge and Kegan Paul, 1979; Compare the argument in Peter Harrison, *'Religion' and the Religions in the English Enlightenment*, Cambridge, Cambridge University Press, 1990.

30 See Michael Fishbane, *Biblical Interpretation in Ancient Israel*, Oxford, The Clarendon Press, 1988.

31 Hartman, 'Criticism and Restitution', in *Tikkun*, vol. 4, February 1989, 29–32.

32 Hartman, *The Unmediated Vision: An Interpretation of Wordsworth, Hopkins, Rilke, and Valery* (1954), New York, Harcourt, Brace & World, Inc., 1966, pp.x–xii,35.

33 'Criticism and Restitution', p. 32.

34 Elie Wiesel, *Souls on Fire and Somewhere a Master*, trans. Marion Wiesel, Harmondsworth, Penguin, 1987, p. 131.

5 POTTER'S FIELD

1 To recapitulate – Phocion was a virtuous Athenian general and statesman, who, like Socrates, was sentenced to die by hemlock, and, in addition, refused burial within the walls of Athens.

2 See *The Age of Alexander: Nine Greek Lives*, trans. Ian Scott-Kilvert, London, Penguin, 1973, pp. 218–51; and Walter Friedlaender, *Poussin:*

A New Approach, London, Thames and Hudson, 1970, p. 176, fig. 74, plate 39.

3 'Literature and the Right to Death', trans. in *The Gaze of Orpheus*, p. 45.

4 *Ibid.*, pp. 45,42.

5 *Le pas au dela*, Paris, Gallimard, 1973, pp. 131–2.

6 The comparison of Orphic and Dionysian religion developed in this paragraph is taken from F. M. Cornford, *From Religion to Philosophy: A Study of the Origins of Western Speculation* (1912), Sussex, Harvester, 1980, pp. 163,195,179,180,196.

7 Compare Michael Platt, 'Looking at Bodies', *International Journal of Philosophy*, vol. 3, 1979, 87–90.

8 Blanchot, *Le pas au dela*, p. 259.

9 *Ibid.*, p. 358, trans. p. 263.

10 Trans. in *The Gaze of Orpheus*, p. 151.

11 *The Writing of the Disaster*, p. 7, trans. p. 1.

12 *Ibid.*, p. 29, trans. p. 14 amended.

13 *Ibid.*, trans. p. 15.

14 *Writing the Disaster*, p. 62.

15 *Phenomenology of Spirit*, p. 244.

16 *Writing the Disaster*, p. 28.

17 *Ibid.*, p. 39 citing Hegel, *Phenomenology*, p. 360.

18 *Ibid.*, p. 59 also citing Hegel, *Phenomenology*, p. 360.

19 *The Writing of the Disaster*, trans. amended.

20 *The Space of Literature*, trans. p. 127.

21 *The Writing of the Disaster*, p. 129, trans. p. 81.

22 'German Memory, Judicial Interrogation, and Historical Reconstruction: Writing Perpetrator History from Postwar Testimony', in Saul Friedlander (ed.), *Probing the Limits of Representation: Nazism and the 'Final Solution'*, Cambridge, MA, Harvard, 1992, pp. 22–36.

INDEX

and mourning, 35–6, 103
and Poussin's *Gathering the
    Ashes of Phocion*, 23–6,
    35
substitution of New Jerusalem
    for, 21–2
versus Jerusalem, 11, 36, 37,
    38, 81
Auschwitz, 123
and Athens, 27, 28–9, 30, 34–5
Borowski's account of, 50
and the devastation of
    knowledge by
    responsibility, 120–1
and Fascism, 59
as fourth city, 26–35
museum, 29–30
in *Schindler's List*, 43, 47
visitors to, 29–30
authority
legal-rational, 15, 58, 88
legitimation of, 4, 5, 9
and Midrash, 78, 86, 96
traditional, 15

Bankier, Abraham, 44
Bar Kochba revolt (135 CE), 84,
    85
Beck, Ulrich, *Risk Society:
    Toward a New
    Modernity*, 59–60
Beckett, Sister Wendy, 22–3, 25,
    26
Benjamin, Walter, 36, 79
'Critique of Violence', 69

*The Origin of German
    Trauerspiel*, 69
'Theses on the Philosophy of
    History', 69
Berlin, *Rosenthaler* gate, 39
Bernal, Martin, 79
Bildung (education, formation,
    cultivation), 72, 74, 75
Blanchot, Maurice, 14
on death, 112–22, 133, 135–7,
    139
and dying as repetition, 106
and the impossibility of dying,
    105–9, 118, 119
'Literature and the Right to
    Death', 115–16, 119
mourning in, 104
and Orphic death, 110–12
'The Two Versions of the
    Imaginary', 112–13
Writing of the Disaster, 116,
    119
Borowski, Tadeusz, *This Way for
    the Gas, Ladies and
    Gentlemen*, 50
broken middles, 38, 42, 75, 76
Browne, Sir Thomas, *Religio
    Medici*, 126–7
Browning, Christopher, 20
Buber, Martin, 99
Buddhist Judaism, 37, 38

Capital (Marx), 66–7
*Capitalism and Rural Society in
    Germany* (Weber), 32